SECOND EDITION - Enlarged

Waifs and Strays of Gaelic Melody

Comprising Forgotten Favorites, Worthy Variants, and Tunes not Previously Printed.

Collected and Edited by

Capt. Francis O'Neill

Compiler and Publisher of

"The Music of Ireland," "The Dance Music of Ireland," and "O'Neill's Irish Music for Piano or Violin."

AUTHOR OF

"Irish Folk Music - A Fascinating Hobby," and "Irish Minstrels and Musicians."

ARRANGED BY

Selena O'Neill, Mus. Bac.

The Mercier Press

Dublin and Cork

THE MERCIER PRESS LIMITED
25 Lower Abbey St., Dublin 1
4 Bridge St., Cork.

Waifs and Strays of Gaelic Melody
ISBN 0 85342 639 2

Printed in the Republic of Ireland by Litho Press Co., Midleton, Co. Cork.

comhaltas ceoltóirí éireann

Cearnóg Belgrave,
Baile na Manach,
Co. Bhaile Átha Cliath

Fon: 800295

CONTINUING THE WORK OF FRANCIS O'NEILL

Tá Proinsias Ó Néill molta dá mbeinnse im thost. Bhí a ainm faoi mheas agus faoi onóir i measc ceoltóirí na hÉireann le linn a sheal, agus is ag dul i méid atá an meas agus an onóir ud ó lá a bháis. Ach is fiú saothar Uí Néill, agus saothar na laoch eile a thug a saol ag obair ar son ceoil agus cultúir na hÉireann a lua agus a ath-mholadh an lá atá inniu ann, mar o tharla an ceol tíre faoi mheas i mbaile agus i gcéin, ní léir do aosóg na linne seo go raibh an ceol ceanna i mbaol a chaillte cúpla scór bliain ó shin. Cúis áthais dúinn mar sin, ceann de leabhra Uí Néill 'Waifs and Strays of Gaelic Melody' – leabhar atá as-chló le fada – a bheith á ath-fhoillsiú ag an Mercier Press.

The publication of Captain Francis O'Neill's several works on Irish music, particularly 'The Dance Music of Ireland' – also known amongst traditional musicians as the 'One Thousand and One' or simply 'The Book' – must rank as one of the most vital influences in the history of Irish traditional music in the 20th century. Another very significant factor was the virtual flood of '78' recordings of artistes such as Paddy Killoran, Tom Morrison, James Morrison and, particularly, of Michael Coleman the great Sligo fiddler. O'Neill's books and the recordings on wax of exiled musicians found their way into thousands of Irish homesteads in the first half of the century. They served as a guide and inspiration in days when it was neither profitable nor socially popular to be involved in discussion on the finer points of reel playing. The country was poor, and racked by apathy and emigration, and Irish musicians were more likely to find a receptive audience in Camden town, Liverpool, New York or Boston than in most Irish towns.

Francis O'Neill had passed on to a better world, – as indeed had Michael Coleman, and that doyen of Irish pipers, Johnny Doran, – when, in 1951, a group of musicians from the Pipers' Club in Thomas Street, Dublin, and from the midland counties, came together to discuss the idea of a national festival of Irish music. O'Neill's writings convey the impression of a man who valued the lore of the music-men as much as he enjoyed the 'swing' and 'lift' of their music. There is no doubt that he would have felt very much at home amongst the ladies and men who gathered for those historic meetings in Mullingar and Dublin in 1951 and '52. It is a matter of record that many of them were well versed in the teachings of the 'Irish musicians' Bible' – O'Neill's 'One Thousand and One.' In the tradition of O'Neill, too, it was their wont to punctuate their labours in the cause of Irish music with enthusiastic sessions of music-making; and worthy sessions they surely were too, for they numbered in their ranks the piping Rowsomes of Dublin, Reynolds, Seery and O Muineacháin of Westmeath, Murray and MacElvaney of Monaghan, musicians from Sligo, Tipperary, Galway, Clare, etc. etc. From those early meetings came the inspiration, and indeed the practical endeavour, which resulted in the first Fleadhanna Cheoil and the rise of Comhaltas Ceoltoiri Eireann.

How close those founder members were to the spirit of O'Neill may be guaged by comparing O'Neill's dedication in 'Waifs and Strays', to No. 4 in the list of Aims and Objects of the newly founded body. The former reads – 'Dedicated to the Spirit of The Gaelic League and The Realisation of its Patriotic Aims': The Comhaltas objective is as follows: 'To co-operate with all bodies working for the restoration of Irish culture.'

Those first members of Comhaltas planned and worked with enthusiasm and diligence. They saw the need for high standards, for research, for publications, for education. They saw, too, the need to preserve the spirit of the music, and the delightful variety and diversity of regional and personal style. The history of Comhaltas, over the past thirty years (1951-1981) may very well seem to those who have been close to it through all or most of those years, as one long, seemingly endless, session of Irish music, with breaks and interludes every now and again for classes, seminars, workshops, summer schools, publications, tours, discussions – each in its own way helping to propagate the 'Ancient Music'. but with the whole providing a pattern and framework and indeed a community where Irish music and Irish culture and folklife can flourish and grow and develop.

Comhaltas Ceoltoiri Eireann from its foundation in 1951, has grown to become a great force in Irish cultural life. Among its achievements are:-

* 40 festivals (fleadhanna cheoil) of Irish traditional music each year;
* 600 classes teaching Irish traditional music;
* Regular courses for beginners, teachers and adjudicators;
* Diploma Course for teachers;
* Fleadh Nua – colourful festival of traditional entertainment;
* Scoil Eigse – Summer College of Irish traditional music, song and dance;
* Tionol Cheoil – recreational/educational weekend at Gormanston College;
* Seisiun na Samhna – a Hallowe'en week-end festival;
* Culturlann na hEireann – Irish Cultural Institute;
* Publication of "Treoir" the magazine of Irish traditional music, song and dance, six times yearly, together with Tutors and other publications;
* Extensive Summer scheme of native entertainment for visitors – over 500 performances;
* Colour film of CCE activities;
* Records of native music and song published each year;
* Annual Cultural Tours of the United States, Canada, Britain and Ireland;
* Extensive scheme of music collection from the older musicians;
* Advisory service on the native culture of Ireland;
* Over 500,000 people attend Comhaltas functions annually.

INTRODUCTION

(Waifs and Strays of Gaelic Melody)

The folk music of Ireland, admittedly richer and more varied than that of any nation, has not only survived the vicissitudes of her tragic history, but has in reality been enriched by countless variants no less pleasing to modern ears than the original strains from which they were derived.

Combined, the Irish and Scotch possess the richest musical inheritance in the world, and so uninterrupted was the intercourse of wandering minstrels between the sister kingdoms—so similar the style of their melodies—that no inconsiderable portion of our finest airs became a sort of disputed property claimed by both peoples.

"No stroke of art their texture bears,
No cadence wrought with learned skill,
And though long worn by rolling years,
Yet unimpaired they please us still;
While thousand strains of mystic lore
Have perished, and are heard no more."

Quoting from a recent issue of **Musical America:** "We start at the folk song, and find in it beauties characteristic of the people who produced it. In our crowded life today there is not much attention paid to it, except by composers in search of material, by artists looking for something novel to exploit, by organizations anxious to see it preserved."

The great composers have gained inspiration from the music of their folk—from melodies created anonymously, or by some whose names do not figure impressively in history, but whose simple, beautiful songs have outlived the passing of generations.

Haydn says "it is the melody which is the charm of music; it is also that which is the most difficult to produce; the invention of a fine melody is a work of genius." Whether it be love or valor, tears or smiles, Irish melody is the inspiring source of all emotions of home, country and faith.

The folk song, passing from father to son, travels far before taking formal shape. It may disappear and crop out in varied form in some other locality, owing to faulty memorizing or difference in vocal or musical ability. Folk music or traditional music is subject to many alterations and the formative influence of many minds. What is beautiful or best remains.

When and by whom the more ancient melodies of Ireland were composed, or how long they have been passed on from one generation to another, are questions not easily answered at this late day, in the absence of positive historical evidence. Perhaps nothing illustrates this more convincingly than the notation "Author and date unknown" which follows the names of 122 of the 149 airs in Bunting's third collection, published in 1840, although 48 of them had been obtained in the last decade of the 18th century.

The late Dr. Joyce, a qualified authority, after making due allowance for duplications and overlapping in the scores of collections of Irish music published down to his day, and including his own, estimated that approximately 3,100 different airs and tunes were recorded in print, and that probably 2,000 more could be sifted from private manuscript collections, and from old people whose memories were stored with strains learned in early life.

A bewildering array of variants and versions greets the musical antiquary on every hand, but the quest for new or distinctly different tunes is certain to involve the assiduous winnowing of much musical chaff.

It is now nearly two centuries since the first printed collection of Irish melodies came from the press. In the year 1726 John and William Neale of Dublin published **A Book of Irish Tunes,** and **A Collection of Irish and Scotch Tunes,** but it must not be forgotten that Playford's **The English Dancing Master,** published from 1651 to 1725, included not a few primitive Irish tunes.

In those days printed music, even if available, could be of little use to the majority of professional Irish musicians, whether harpers, pipers, or fiddlers, who, having lost their sight by the ravages of small pox before the days of vaccination, had no choice but that of music as a vocation.

Under such circumstances it is obvious that imperfect memorizing of tunes acquired from oral instruction, or picked up promiscuously from the lilting or playing of others, accounts in part at least for the wealth of variants of well known airs and tunes traceable to a common origin, and the farther back they are traced the simpler and more skeletonic we find them. Skilful instrumentalists have in process of time embellished the framework or theme with an embroidery of graces and varied finishes, which go far to relieve the monotony of melodies ordinarily consisting of but eight bars in each part, and in some instances only four bars repeated.

The charm of dance music does not end with the rhythmic requirements of the dancer, for although jigs, reels, and hornpipes, were primarily composed to be accompanied by dancing, they have been in many instances wedded to song. By no means few are the examples known to us, which, played in slow time, are susceptible of much expression and beauty. Perceval Graves' "Father O'Flynn," set to the tune of "The Top of Cork Road," is a conspicuous example.

The psychologist may understand why the rhythm or swing of an Irish or Scotch reel, or other Gaelic dance tune, so vitally affects the average audience, which listens unmoved to the strains of much more pretentious compositions. "Melody is truly the soul of music," remarked Sir John Graham Dalzell in 1781. "I have been twice present at convivial entertainments when the best compositions by the most celebrated performers were heard without emotion. Yet the moment an excellent, lively and inspiring tune—Mrs. McLeod of Raasay's reel—commenced, a party of dancers started up to enjoy it; nor was this a novelty." Nor are such incidents a novelty today.

Although no less than thirty collections of Irish music, whole or in part, were published in the three kingdoms in the 18th century, comparatively few dance tunes are to be found among their contents. Several collections of **Scots Reels or Country Dances** were issued in parts by Robert Bremner in Edinburgh from 1757 to 1768. Neil Stewart, John Riddle, Daniel Dow and at least a dozen others followed his example before the end of the century. In all of them are to be found certain tunes in common circulation in Ireland.

INTRODUCTION

It appears that the gentle art of plagiarising tunes is no modern foible, for we have it on the authority of the editor of the **Glen Collection of Scottish Dance Music** that the practice of changing a few notes in a coveted tune, and renaming it as one's own, led to much ill feeling and endless confusion. The chief offenders in that line of perfidy, strange to relate, were the celebrated Neil Gow and his sons, their principal victim being William Marshall, butler and house steward to the Duke of Gordon, "the most brilliant as well as the most prolific composer of strathspey music Scotland ever produced."

A fair sprinkling of Irish airs and dance tunes graces the pages of **A Selection of Scotch, English, Irish and Foreign Airs,** issued in six parts from 1782 to 1797 by John Aird of Glasgow.

The pioneer publication of Irish dance music—**Jackson's Celebrated Irish Tunes**—came from the press in 1774, but while many of "Piper" Jackson's jigs, and a few of his hornpipes, are well known to traditional Irish musicians, it is doubtful if a copy of his work exists today outside the files of Dublin museums. None of Jackson's tunes are included in **The Hibernian Muse,** published by J. and W. Thompson at London in 1787. Instead, special prominence is given to Carolan's compositions.

Another Irish piper named O'Farrell, who figured prominently on the London stage late in the 18th century, published three creditable collections of Irish airs and dance tunes, flavored with a few choice Scotch selections by way of variety. **O'Farrell's Collection of National Music for the Union Pipes, etc.,** appeared in 1797, followed by **O'Farrell's Pocket Companion for the Irish or Union Pipes, etc.,** two volumes, in four parts, 1800 to 1810.

Bunting virtually ignored dance tunes. Among the 295 numbers in his three Collections—1796, 1809, 1840—possibly ten may be considered as of that class, although but three tunes are so named. The same may be said of **Moore's Irish Melodies,** the majority of which were taken from Bunting's first and second Collections.

Of the 1582 numbers (376 of them anonymous) in the Stanford edition of **The Complete Collection of Irish Music as noted by George Petrie LL.D.; R.H.A.;** published for the Irish Literary Society of London, 1902-5, about ten per cent are of the dance tune variety. Less than fifteen per cent of the contents of the Joyce Collections may be considered of the same class. In other words, of the 2819 numbers in the Bunting, Petrie and Joyce Collections combined, 300 or about eleven per cent would be a liberal estimate of the tunes which may be regarded as jigs, reels, hornpipes, or long-dances. Furthermore, it is well to remember that hundreds of variants are strewn through the pages of these collections, especially the two last named.

The great disparity between the number of airs, and dance tunes in such noted collections, plainly indicates that the former are the more ancient and diversified, because singing is a universal accomplishment, while skill in instrumental music is limited, and of comparatively recent development. It is quite apparent also that an appreciable number of dance tunes have been evolved from airs and marches, since the Irish or Union bagpipe and fiddle supplanted the harp in the latter half of the 18th century.

Whether attributable to the versatility of traditional musicians in composing new tunes, or the untiring diligence of modern collectors, the fact remains that more than 1200 classified dance tunes are recorded in the O'Neill Collections, published in 1903 and later years. The majority of them were noted down from the playing of the pipers, fiddlers, and fluters of the famous Irish Music Club of Chicago.

Compositions of another class, called Planxties in Ireland, and ports in Scotland, were in vogue in the heyday of the harpers, especially Carolan. Port or **puirt** is the Gaelic word for jig, but the genesis of Planxty, variable in metre and tempo, has not been clearly defined. Both, however, were composed in honor of generous and hospitable patrons, who have been immortalized in the names of the tunes. All that survived of the planxties have been preserved in print, but their popularity has been on the wane for a long time.

The optimism of Dr. Joyce was hardly justified by the results obtained by the Irish Feis Ceoil Association from the "vast amount of material" comprised in the many manuscript collections of music awarded prizes in 1897, and several years thereafter. So much of the contents was found to be duplicated in the Petrie, Joyce, and other collections, that by a tedious process of elimination there remained but 85 unpublished melodies to grace the pages of **The Feis Ceoil Collection of Irish Airs,** which came from the press in 1914.

Following the suggestions of Dr. Joyce in the preface to **Old Irish Folk Music and Songs,** a critical examination of manuscript music obtained from such divergent sources as Ireland, England, Australia, and various States of the Union, disclosed little but variants of melodies previously published. That little, however, was too good to be lost. To this aggregation of **Waifs and Strays** have been added selections gleaned from rare volumes of the 18th century and later, which are practically inaccessible to the public in this generation.

There remains but the pleasant duty of acknowledging our obligations to kindred spirits, inspired by a unity of musical sentiment, who manifested their helpfulness in various practical ways.

With a view to according due recognition, the names of contributors of tunes, or the sources from which they were obtained, follow the titles of all numbers in this work. Certain exceptionally important contributions to the cause, call for special mention even at the sacrifice of other considerations.

Of the manuscript collections available through the kindness of musical compatriots, the most valuable was one which included much of the repertory of Jeremiah Breen, a blind fiddler of great repute who flourished a generation ago in North Kerry, between Listowel and Ballybunion. His tunes were noted down by Thomas Rice, a talented pupil, and later copied by his friend James P. Walsh, now a Sergeant of police in Chicago. From a mutual friend, Richard Sullivan, a much admired dancer hailing from the same locality, came the information that the Sergeant's precious manuscript had passed into the possession of Patrick Stack, a fiddler whose execution was no less admirable than his modesty. Not only did this knight of the bow favor the writer with the custody of the Rice-Walsh Manuscript, so-called, but he obligingly wrote out settings of several of his own rare tunes which had so far escaped all collectors.

Another manuscript collection found among Sergeant James O'Neill's accumulations yielded some choice selections penned in 1878-9 by an enthusiast named Humphrey Murphy. A fragment of a nameless discolored collection of time-worn tunes—mainly waltzes and polkas—from the same source, rewarded investigation with a few rarities.

No formal expression of appreciation could do justice to the unselfish co-operation of Francis E. Walsh of San Francisco, Cal. A member of the one-time famous Irish Music Club of Chicago, Mr. Walsh, with the skill, patience and tact so essential to his task, scored in musical notation many fine variants and unpublished tunes as played by clever fiddlers, and fluters, now residing in that city. From the storehouse of his own memory he added other favored numbers, and generously forwarded the total to the Editor in the interest of Irish musical regeneration.

For years the correspondence of Dr. H. C. Mercer of Doylestown, Pa., was an intellectual stimulant. Curator of the Bucks County Historical Society, Dr. Mercer is also an enthusiast on folk music, both Gaelic and American. Quotations from his published articles on the latter, are included in the descriptive text. To his generosity we owe the historical pictures "The Blind Fiddler" and "Lochaber No More", printed from blocks supplied at his personal expense.

As a sixth and final contribution to the cherished cause of perpetuating Gaelic musical tradition, the compilation of this work—unique in many respects—was undertaken in the sunset years of a long and adventurous life, and at a time when the difficulties of publication were most discouraging.

Should the musical antiquary, or modern composer derive from a study of **Waifs and Strays of Gaelic Melody** as much profit, as the editor did of pleasure in its compilation and publication, all is well, and the desired end has been attained.

August 28, 1922.

CLASSIFIED INDEX

As a preliminary word, "The" is omitted in names of Airs or Tunes in the index. For example; in looking for "The Knight of St. Patrick Lancers," the name will be found under the letter K in the Class of Special Dances.

AIRS—SONGS

CLASSIFIED INDEX

AIRS—SONGS

MARCHES *and* MISCELLANEOUS

SPECIAL DANCES

DOUBLE JIGS

SLIP or HOP JIGS

REELS

HORNPIPES

THE BLIND FIDDLER

Painting by Sir David Wilkie, born in Scotland, 1785

Planxty Toby Peyton

Sergt. Jas. O'Neill

Moderato con expressivo

1

mf *p* *ff* *p*

Among the compositions of Carolan the last of the Bards, noted down by Edward Bunting at the Belfast Harp Festival in 1792, was "Planxty Toby Peyton," as played by Hugh Higgins; but it was not published until his third collection, *The Ancient Music of Ireland* appeared in 1840.

Bunting's setting with two others of distinctly different arrangement, was printed in *O'Neills Music of Ireland, Chicago, 1903*. The third setting which is here reproduced was known to John McFadden hailing from County Mayo, and to Sergt. Jas. O'Neill from County Down. Both had learned the tune in practically identical notation in their youth, and both played it in a style to indicate that whoever evolved the flowing rhythmic variant from the Bard's original composition, was a versatile musical genius.

Young Terence McDonough

Carolan

2

Andante

As "McDonogh's Lamentation" this fine air composed by Carolan in 1696 on the death of a famous young Catholic lawyer of Sligo, was printed in *The Hibernian Muse, London, 1787*. Bunting included it under the above name in *The General Collection of the Ancient Irish Music, Dublin 1796*. An identical version of it but in a different key appears in *Clinton's Gems of Ireland, London, 1841*. A poem by Sir Walter Scott entitled "The Return to Ulster" is set to this air in *Thomson's Select Collection of Original Irish Airs, Edinburgh, 1814-16*. It is also to be found in *Smith's Irish Minstrel, Edinburgh 1825* as the air of "The Moon Dimmed Her Beams." a poem by an unknown author. McDonogh was the first Catholic permitted to practice law under the penal laws.

Rocking the Cradle

Sergt. Jas. O'Neill

3

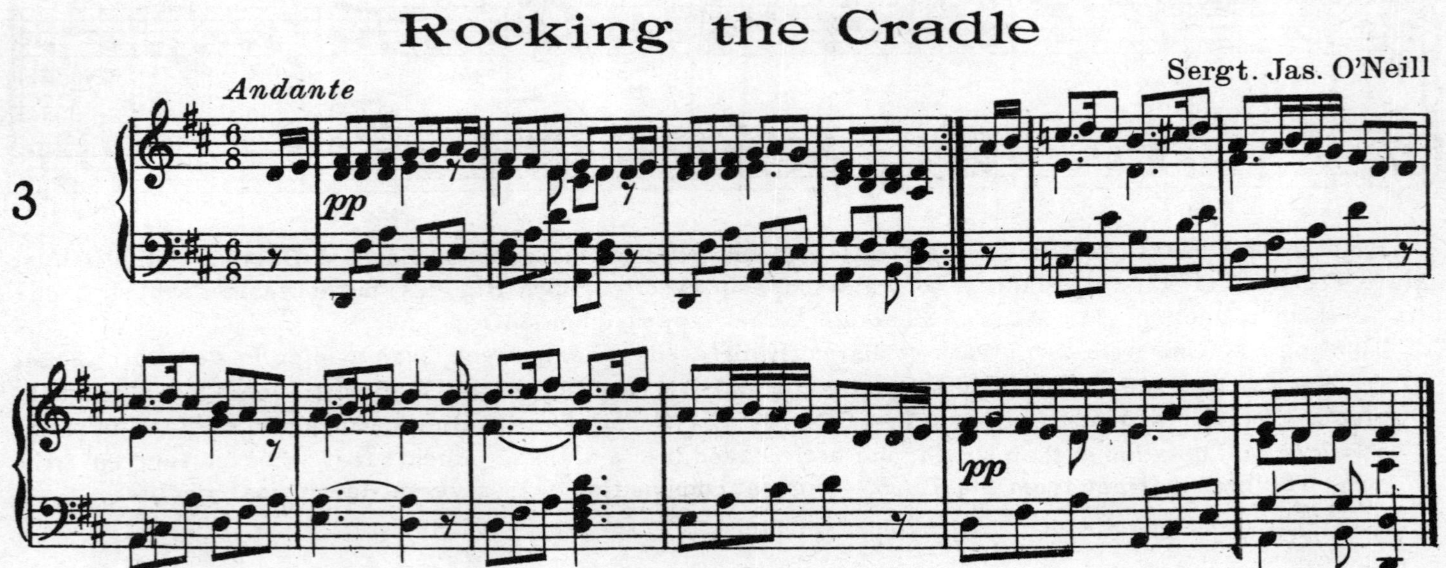

The Old Man Rocking the Cradle

Rice-Walsh Mss.

Few of what are termed "descriptive pieces" had such a vogue in Ireland a few generations ago as one variously named "Rocking the Cradle"; "The Old Man Rocking the Cradle"; and "Rocking a Baby that's None of My Own."

In a querulous plaintive strain the mismated old man gives voice to his woes, punctuated by the wailing of a peevish child, and its calls for its Ma-ma. Skilful Irish pipers and fiddlers, particularly the latter successfully imitate those accompaniments. To bring out the tones approaching human expression, the fiddle is lowered in pitch, and the fiddler holding a long old fashioned door key firmly between the teeth lightly touched the bridge of his instrument with it at appropriate passages. Those expert in manipulation produced very amusing if not edifying results.

"I Sat in the Vale" a poem by H. S. Riddell is set to the air "The Rocking of the Cradle" in *Smith's The Irish Minstrel, Edinburgh 1825.* The melody is essentially the same as Sergt. O'Neill's setting. The air does not appear by name at least in the Bunting, Petrie, or Joyce Collections.

One Bottle More

Moderato Sergt. Jas. O'Neill

5

In *O'Farrell's Pocket Companion for the Irish or Union Pipes 1804-10* we find the above tune in a slightly different setting

Teddy O'Néill

Andante Rice-Walsh. Mss.

6

The Willow Tree

Andante Miss Lucy Ray

7

I Was Roaming in the Gloaming

Jas. Whiteside. Mss.

Irish Lament for Martyred Soggarth Aroon
Jas. Whiteside. Mss.
Adagio con expressione
10
Irish Widow's Lament on the Death of Her Only Son
Jas. Whiteside. Mss.
Andante
11

Limerick's Lamentation

Bunting's Arrangement 1809.

Adagio

12

f

p

mf

p

tr

As far back as the year 1676 this melody was referred to as "The Irish Tune." The earliest printed setting of the air bearing the title "Limbrick's Lamentation," appeared in *Daniel Wright's Aria di Camera — Being a Collection of Scotch, Irish, and Welsh Airs* published about 1730. An almost identical setting was printed in *The Hibernian Muse*, published by S.A.& P. Thompson, London 1787. "Limerick's Lamentation" is one of the numbers in *Bunting's General Collection of the Ancient Music of Ireland, London 1809* but the arrangement differs so materially from that presented in *McCullagh's Collection of Irish Airs* published in Dublin 1821, that both are submitted for comparison as one of many instances which lead us to believe that there were few if any standards but those of individual taste, or preference in the settings or versions of Irish airs or tunes. Stevenson's arrangement of this air to Moore's song, "When Cold in the Earth" is in the Key of b flat.

Limerick's Lamentation

LIMERICK'S LAMENTATION (Concl.)

Lochaber No More

"Farewell to Lochaber, Farewell to My Jean"

Andante Moderato *Caledonian Muse London 1785*

14

Concerning the disputed claims to priority of the above, and "Limerick's Lamentation," perhaps no better authority can be adduced than Alfred Moffat, author of *The Minstrelsy of Scotland;* and *The Minstrelsy of Ireland.* In a footnote page 300 of the latter work we read: "Thomas Duffet's song 'Since Coelia's my foe' published in that author's *New Poems London 1676,* is marked, 'Song to the Irish Tune;' there is no music in this work, but in the *Lover's Opera 1730,* we find the air designated 'Since Coelia's my foe' to be the tune claimed by the Irish as 'Limerick's Lament', and by the Scotch as 'Lochaber no more'. We may therefore fairly presume that as far back as 1676— that is— just fifty years prior to the appearance of *Ramsay's Tea Table Miscellany* vol. II, in which 'Lochaber' was first printed, the air was known as an Irish tune."

The air or melody published with Ramsay's song in *Thomson's Orpheus Caledonius London, 1733,* varies considerably both in composition and number of bars, from the setting herewith presented.

Among other notables glorified in an anonymous Irish song was a King Philip of Spain whose aid was hoped for. We find nothing in the life of the monarch to arouse the enthusiastic toast "Here's a health to the gallant King Philip," as translated by Dr. George Sigerson. There is no record of the composer's name. Three versions of this fine melody are submitted for the purpose of illustrating the tendency of time and talent to favor the creation of variants of popular compositions. It may be added that the setting in *The Hibernian Muse* published in London 1787 is nearly identical with that in *Burk Thumoth's Collection*, and differs not materially from a setting in The Stanford—Petrie Collection of Irish Music without note or comment. The editor has taken the liberty of correcting the Irish titles as printed in the originals.

Slainte Righ Pilib

(Health to King Philip)

Burk Thumoth's
12 Scotch and 12 Irish Airs 1743

15

Slainte Righ Pilib

Kate Kearney with Variations

Tempo di Valse

Capt. F. O'Neill

Long before Lady Morgan wrote the words of "Kate Kearney," the melody was known. As "The Beardless Boy" it was printed in *Bunting's General Collection of The Anciant Irish Music 1796* and again as "The Dissipated Youth" in *A General Collection of The Ancient Music of Ireland* published in 1809. In the latter year it appeared also as "Kate Martin" in *Murphy's Irish Airs and Jigs*. As a waltz tune Kate Kearney lacked a sufficiently distinct second part, which some orchestra leader eventually supplied. This though serviceable for the purpose intended is devoid of any trace of Irish feeling.

Drimen Duff

(Druim fionn dubh)

Burk Thumoth 12 Scotch and 12 Irish Airs, 1742.

Andante Expressivo.

19

To many persons such names as Drimenduff, Drimin dhuv, Drimindoo, Drimindhu, Drimin dhoun, Drimin dhoun deelish, etc; convey but little if any meaning. A few words of explanation may not be superfluous.

Much more common among cattle in former times than since distinct breeds had been developed, was a white stripe extending along the spine of black or brown cows. This peculiarity of coloration was termed in Irish, *Druim-fionn,* or white-back, and became by aspiration Drimmin or Drimen. Hence we have Drimmin-fionn-dubh, (Drimmin-dhuv) or white-back black cow; Druim-fionn-donn, (Drimmin dhoun) or white-back brown cow, and so on with related names.

In poetical literature those titles are allegorical. "Drimmin Dhu" was a political password among the Irish Jacobites, and all "Drimmin" songs - by no means few - breathe a spirit of fealty to the Jacobite cause.

Drimmin Dhoun Oge

(Druim-fionn donn og)

O'Farrell's Pocket
Companion 1804-10.

Andantino.

20

p *f* *ff* *p* *fz*

Lament of the Arran Fishermen

Andante con Expression.

Seamus Moriarty
San Francisco.

21

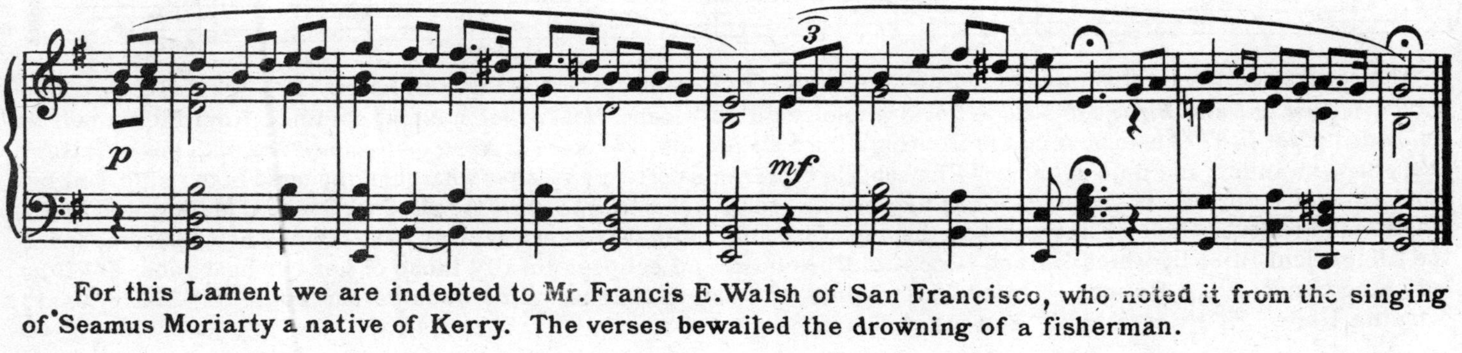

p *mf* *p* *mf*

For this Lament we are indebted to Mr. Francis E. Walsh of San Francisco, who noted it from the singing of Seamus Moriarty a native of Kerry. The verses bewailed the drowning of a fisherman.

Father Tom O'Neill

Con Spirito. Capt. F. O'Neill.

A ballad extending to 19 verses sung to this air recited the conspiracy of an infatuated wealthy heiress in County Armagh to inveigle or coerce a young clergyman the son of a widow, into matrimony; and the frustration of her designs by the confession of an accomplice. The melody hitherto unpublished I believe, has clung to my memory since childhood.

Graine Uaile
(Grace O'Malley)

Slow and with feeling. *O'Farrell's Pocket Companion 1804-10.*

23

mp cresc. mf f ff

The earliest setting of this famous old air which the editor could trace was that printed in *O'Farrell's Pocket Companion for the Irish or Union Pipes. 1804-10.* A florid version entitled "Granu Weal or ma-ma-ma", obtained from McDonnell a renowned piper in 1797 is to be found in Bunting's third Collection, *The Ancient Music of Ireland-1840,* with the notation, "Very ancient, author and date unknown." The subtitle represents certain passages wherein a repeated note reinforced by concords on the regulators produced tones like ma-ma-ma. *Grainne ni Mhaille* — Anglicized Grace O'Malley—who flourished in the reign of Queen Elizabeth was the most forceful character of her day. Her Irish maiden name became one of the allegorical titles by which Ireland is poetically known, and eclipses totally those of her two husbands, O'Flaherty, and Sir Richard Bourke. In course of time, the original Irish name became corrupted to "Granu Weal," "Graina Uaile," "Grainu Mhaol," and other forms.

Did You See My Man Looking for Me?

Moderato spiritoso.

Capt. F. O'Neill.

24

mf
f
pp
f

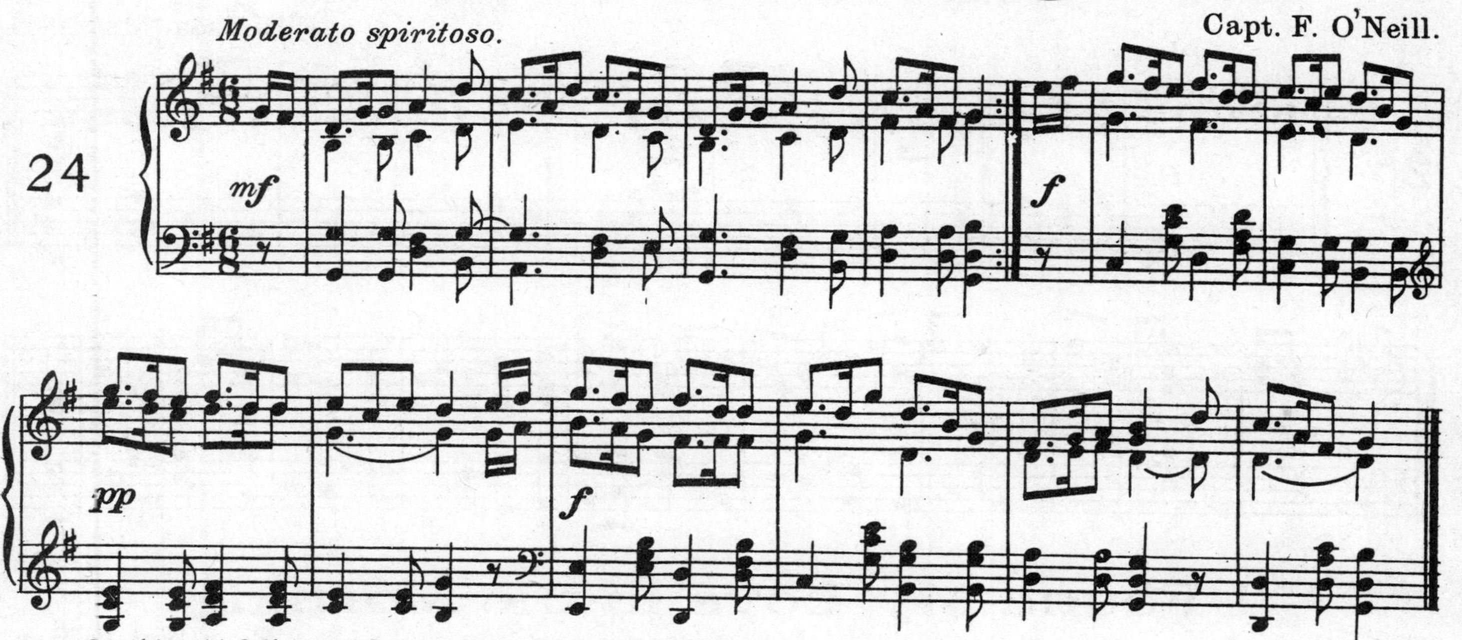

Of this old folk song I remember the following verse:

Did you see my man, he was a fine man?
Did you see my man looking for me?
He wore a green jacket a pair of white stockings,
A hump on his back and he's blind of one eye;
A corduroy breeches; his brogues full of stitches-
Did you see my man looking for me?

Sweet Castle Hill

Andante.

P. J. Healy San Francisco.

25

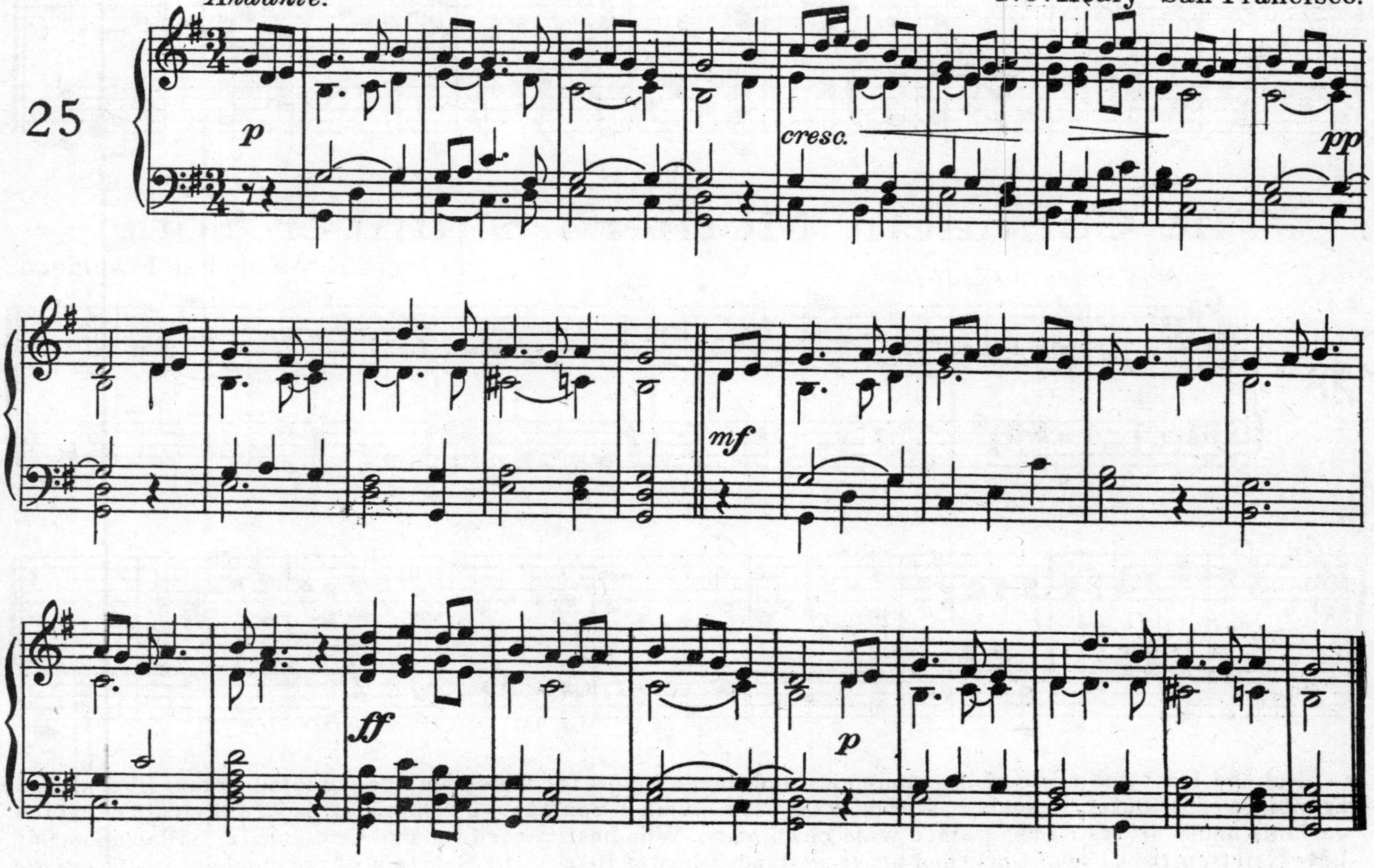
p
cresc.
pp
mf
ff
p

Go My Own Darling Boy

Not the least charming of the many airs and dance tunes, for which we are indebted to our liberal San Francisco contributor, Francis E. Walsh, is the fine Slumber Song above printed. It is an old strain of which variants under divers names gained wide circulation. Who hasn't heard the one time popular ballad about "My Love Nell from the Cove of Cork" and her inconstancy. "Mary of Blackwater Side" one of the numbers in *Joyce's Old Irish Folk Music and Songs Dublin 1909* betrays a similar origin.

The Battle of Aughrim

Walker's Historical Memoirs of the Irihs Bards, London 1786

To the musical antiquary war cries, and battle pieces, may be not without interest. To the modern ear they possess but little attraction; yet when Martin O'Reilly the blind piper from Galway at the Dublin Feis in 1901 played a descriptive selection entitled "The Battle of Aughrim" (1691) in which the blare of trumpets, battle onslaught, and wailing of the women were imitated, his performance was rapturously applauded.

The Lamentation of Aughrim

Andantino *McCullagh's Collection of Irish Airs, Dublin 1821*

30

p *pp* *mf*

At the battle of Aughrim July 12th 1691, fought near Ballinasloe, County Galway, General St. Ruth in command of the Irish forces, and 7,000 of his troops were killed.

The Cuckoo

Miss Lucy Ray

Moderato
31
p
f
p

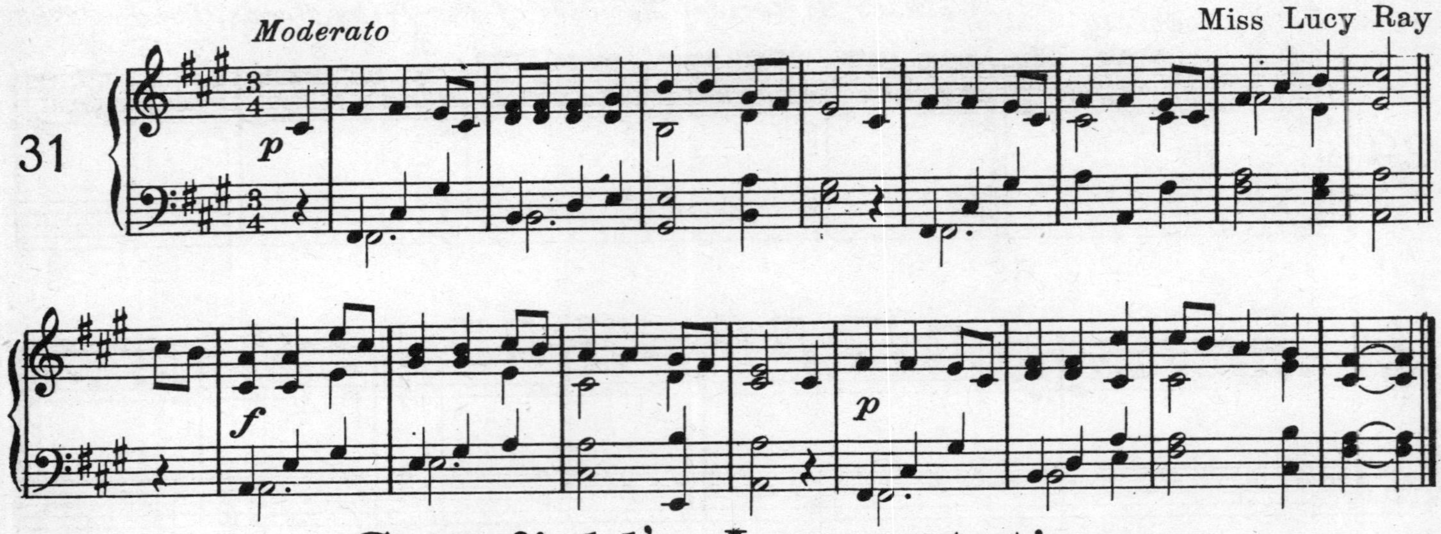

Sarsfield's Lamentation

The Hibernian Muse, London 1787

Andante sostenuto
32
p
f
p
pp
f
cresc.
p

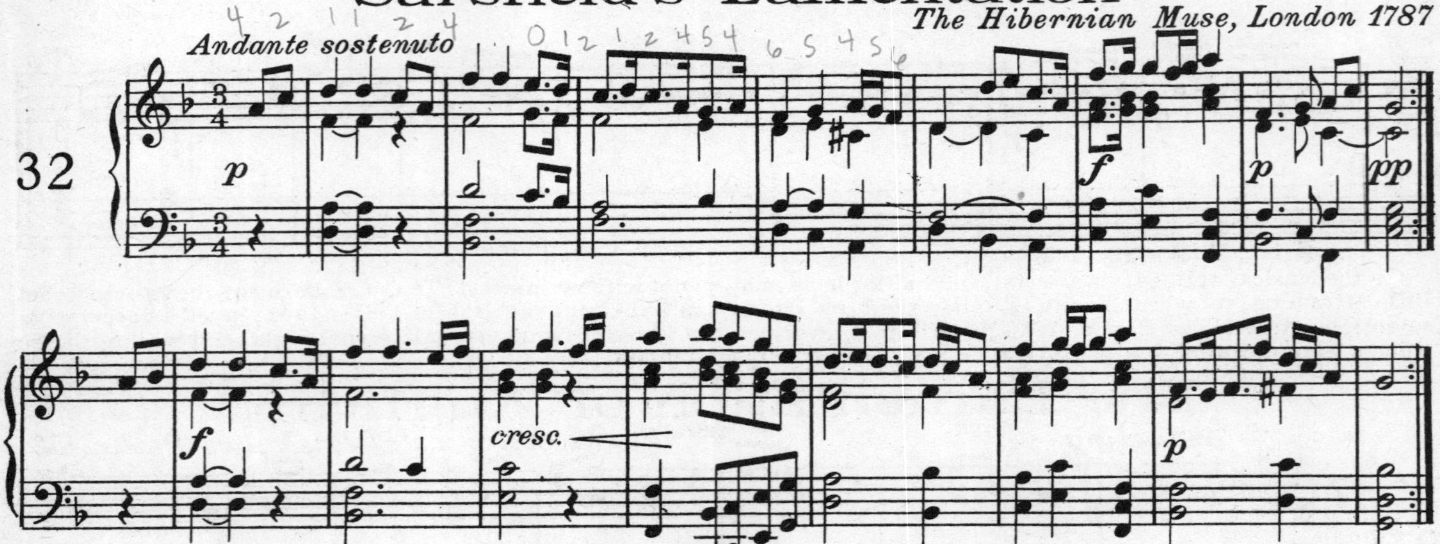

This Lamentation published in *The Hibernian Muse, London 1787* derives its importance from the historical prominence of General Sarsfield as the Irish Commander at the Seige of Limerick. That circumstance obviously accounts for its being confounded in later times with "Limerick's Lamentation." This composition bears no resemblance except in name to the "Lament for Sarsfield." No. 433, *O'Neill's Music of Ireland, Chicago, 1903*.

The Dark-eyed Gipsy

P. J. Healey, San Francisco.

Andante
33
p

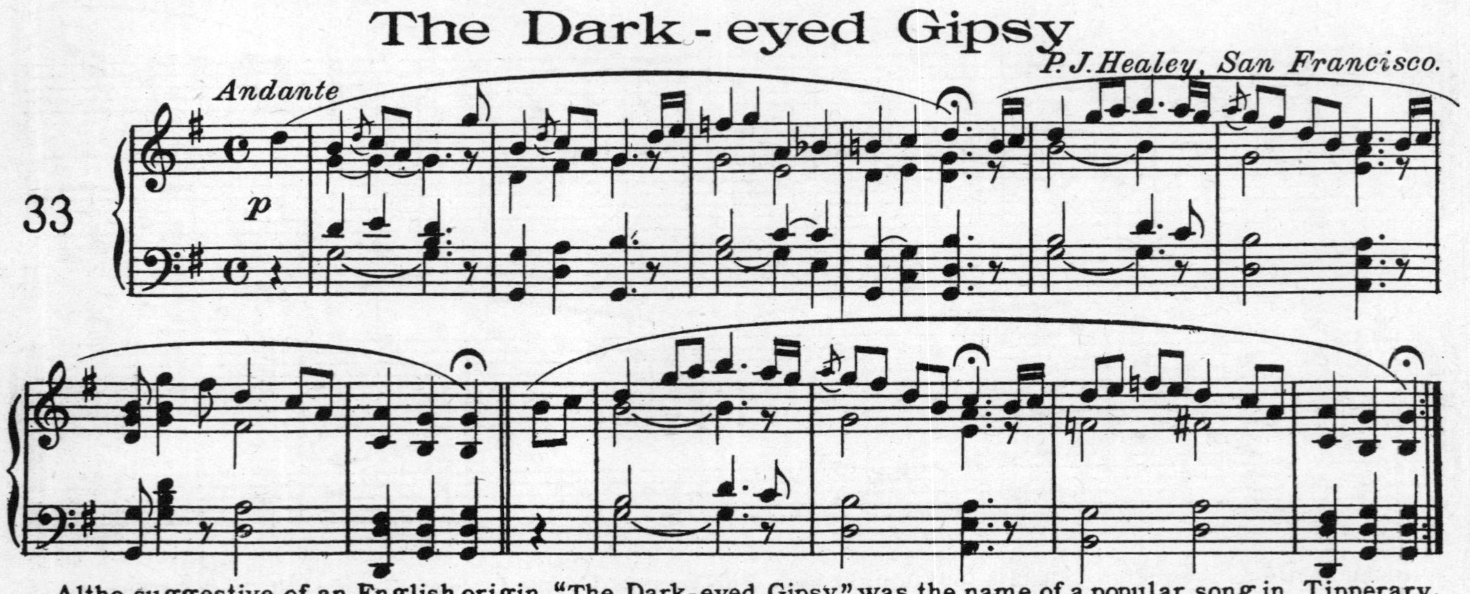

Altho suggestive of an English origin, "The Dark-eyed Gipsy" was the name of a popular song in Tipperary, Mr. Healey's native county.

(Hill of Usnach)

P. J. O'Donohue.
San Francisco.

I am informed by our liberal contributor Mr. Francis E. Walsh of San Francisco, that variants of the above air are known to several of his musical acquaintances but by different names, such as "Knuck Usnach Gathering;" "Knuck Costhnach;" "The Coming of Lugh;" and "The Poor Man's Friend." Mr. O'Donohue whose setting is presented insists that it is the true air of "Willy Reilly" the old time favorite of an earlier generation. The melody is the real thing however.

Molly of Lough Erne Shore

James Whiteside Mss.

Andante.

35

p *pp* *f*

The Gay Young Fireman

Capt. F. O'Neill.

Moderato.

36

mf

Some fifty years ago I heard a ballad sung to this air by a young lady hailing from Brooklyn, N.Y. It recited the fascinations of A Gay Young Fireman of that city. The strain, unmistakably of Irish origin displays marked individuality.

My Dear Irish Girl

Con Spirito. Capt. F. O'Neill.

37

mf 3

p

f

Not a few songs or ballads have been sung to a variant of this old air, one of them being named "The Hat My Father Wore," where the second part came from the Editor is unable to say, except that it has lodged in his memory for many years.

The Dawning of the Day

Aird's Selections 1782-97.

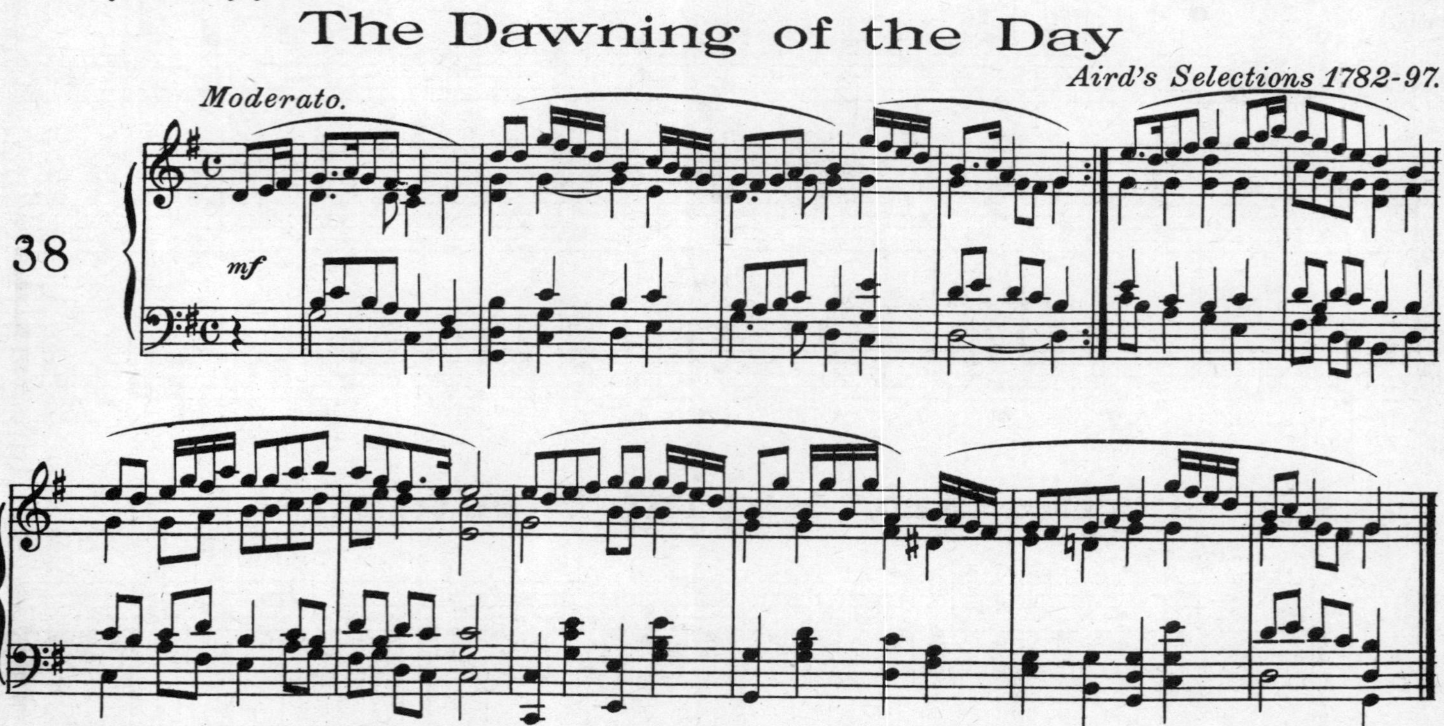

This fine air, the best known of the compositions of the great harper Thomas O'Connellan was taken from *Aird's Selection of Scotch, English, Irish, and Foreign Airs, Vol. 3,* published in 1788. O'Connellan flourished in a period when the renown of Irish harpers became a matter of history. After a sojourn of 20 years in Scotland, he returned to his native land in 1689, and died nine years later. As the above Setting differs materially from that of Bunting in his Second Collection issued in 1809, and others much more recent, its introduction among *Waifs and Strays* may be not without interest to students of Irish musical history.

The Lamentation of Owen Roe O'Neill

Carolan

This fine composition is attributed to Carolan in *Bunting's General Collection of the Ancient Irish Music, Dublin 1796*; *Hardiman's Irish Minstrelsy, London 1831*; and *Clinton's Gems of Ireland, London 1841*. Grattan Flood an eminent authority states in his *A History of Irish Music, Dublin, 1905*, that this "glorious 'Lament' was composed on the death of Owen Roe O'Neill in 1649," a date preceding Carolan's birth by twenty-one years. Owen Roe O'Neill, prince of Ulster, was a gallant military leader who vanquished the British forces at the battle of Benburb in 1646.

Jessie the Flower of Dunblane

Wood's Songs of Scotland, Edinburgh 1848

* Early in the nineteenth century this song was composed by a modest weaver Robert Tannahill of Paisley, and was set to an alleged ancient Scottish melody, by Robert A. Smith author of the *Irish Minstrel*, and the *Scottish Minstrel*. According to Farquhar Graham editor of *Woods Song of Scotland*, not a few of the airs in the latter work were composed by Smith himself. Whatever the origin of the above melody may have been it has a decidedly Gaelic tonality.

O'Connell's Lamentation

Sergt. Jas. O'Neill

41

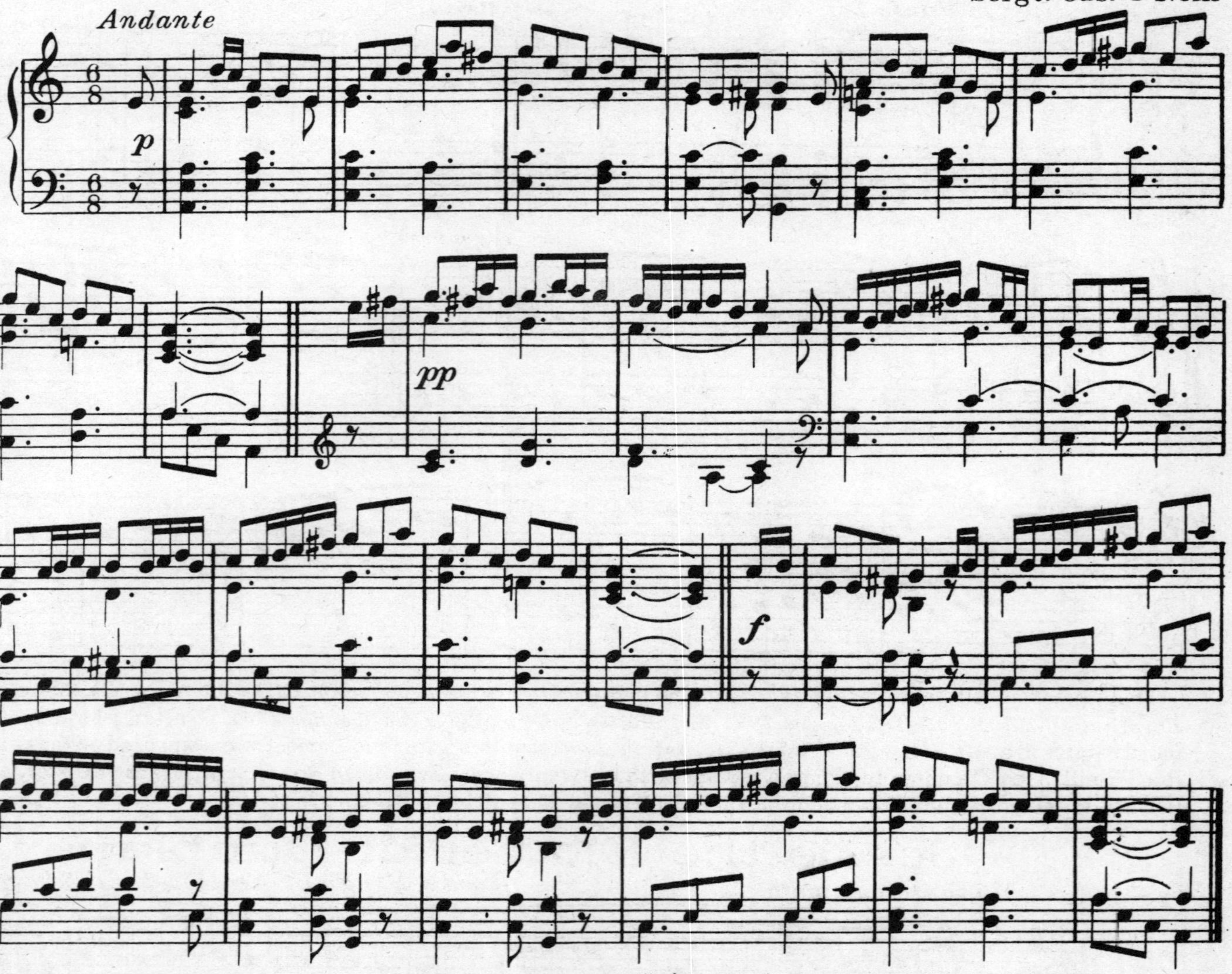
Andante
p
pp
f

Comparing very favorably with compositions of this class. "O'Connell's Lamentation" is presented as the production of two members of the once famous Irish Music Club of Chicago which flourished in the early years of the twentieth century. The first and second parts were outlined by John McFadden an untutored fiddler of fertile fancy, and dextrous execution. The third part as well as the whole arrangement is the work of Sergt. James O'Neill, the Club's worthy scribe.

All I Want is a Decent Boy

O'Farrell's Pocket Companion 1804-10

42

Andantino
f
p

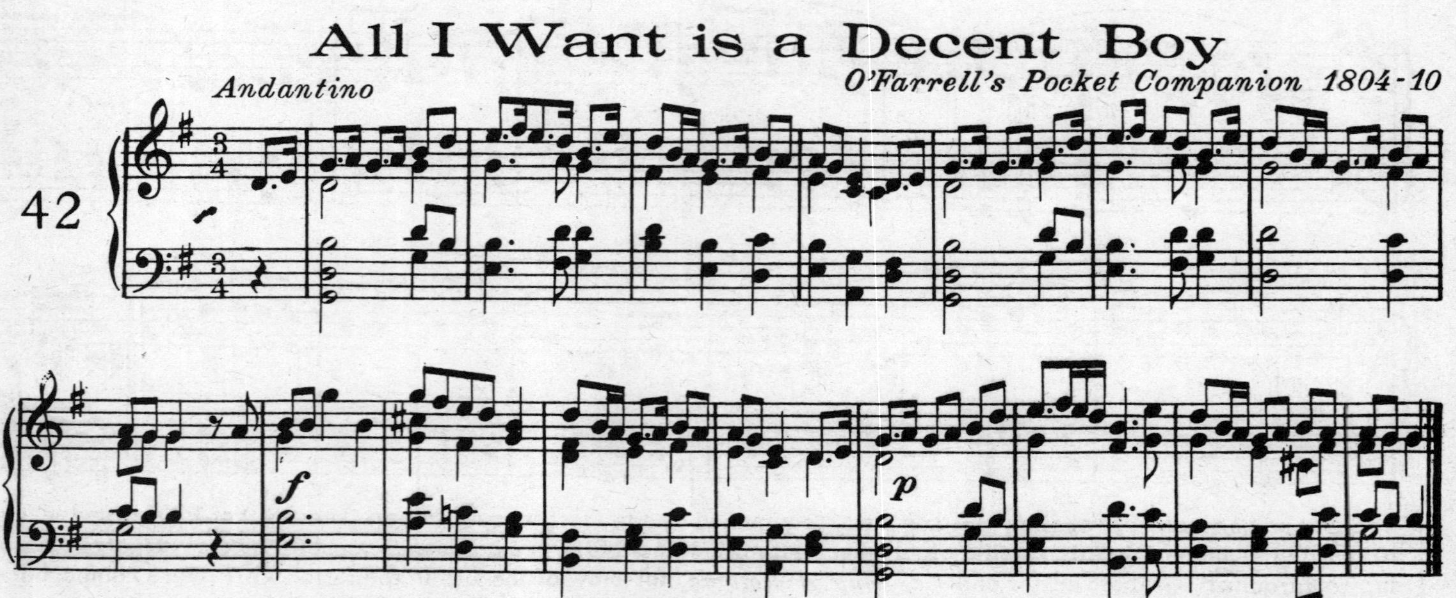

The name of a ballad sung to this air has been substituted for "The Young Man's Dream"—an obviously wrong title—as printed in O'Farrell's work.

Captain O'Kain, or The Wounded Hussar.

McGoun's Repository, 1803.

Moderato.

43

p mf cresc. ff dim. pp

The earliest setting of this rare composition which the compiler can trace is that found in vol.3 of *Aird's Selections of Scotch, English, Irish, and Foreign Airs,* printed in 1788. Slightly disguised as "Captain Oakhain: A Favourite Irish Tune," it appears in *McGoun's Repository of Scots and Irish Airs, Strathspeys, Reels, etc; Glasgow, 1803,* but it is not numbered among the Bunting, or Petrie Collections. "The Wounded Hussar" we learn from Alexander Campbell's song of that name printed with the music in *Smith's Irish Minstrel, Edinburgh, 1825,* was Cap't. Henry O'Kain who died of his wounds on "the banks of the dark rolling Danube." Included as one of Carolan's compositions in *Hardiman's Irish Minstrelsy, 1831,* the author adds: "Capt. O'Kane or O'Cahan of a distinguished family, a sporting Irishman well known in Antrim in his day as 'Slasher O'Kane!'" There can be no doubt that he was the hero of Campbell's song. "The Wounded Hussar" is also included in Surenne's *Songs of Ireland without words. Edinburgh 1854.*

Young Ellen of My Heart.

Rice–Walsh Mss.

This air like scores of others was unconsciously memorized in my boyhood days at Tralibane some three miles southeast of Bantry, West Cork. All that I can remember now of the ballad sung to it is the distich:

"My true love he has gone from me, and I can't tell how far—
Eighteen hundred thousand miles, on board of a man of war!"

It is not likely that the poetaster in equalizing his meter, realized the absurdity of a voyage equal to seventy-two times the circumference of the earth.

My Only Joe and Deary O.

Maestoso. *Wilson's Companion to the Ball Room, London, 1816.*

47

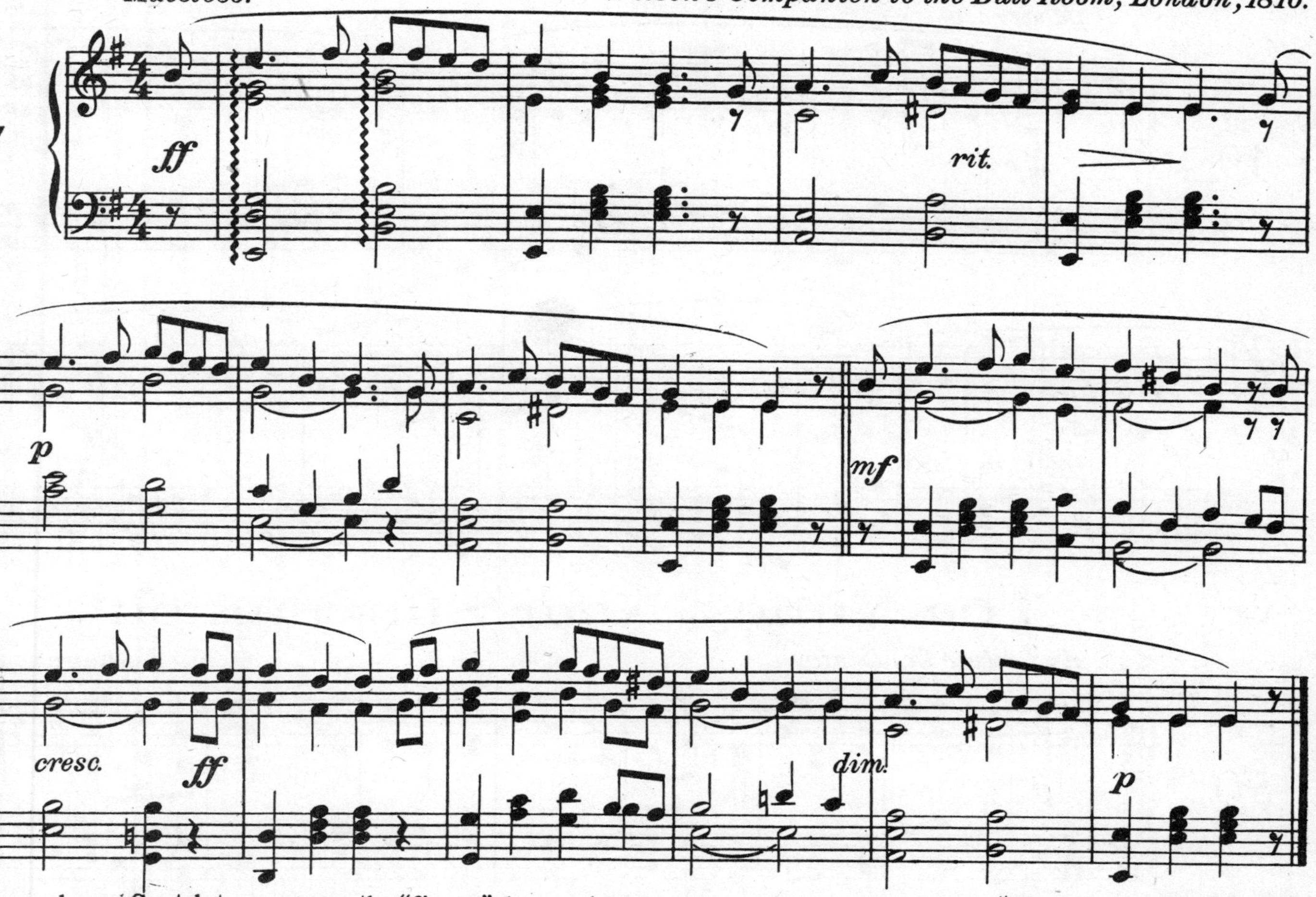

Classed as a Scotch tune among the "figure" dances in *Wilson's Companion to the Ball Room* "My Only Joe and Deary O," is not listed in the Analytical Table of *The Glen Collection of Scottish Dance Music, Strathspeys, Reels, and Jigs, Edinburgh, 1891.* It is quite distinct however from "My Ain Kind Dearie" first printed in the 12th Number of *Robert Bremner's Collection of Scots Reels or Country Dances* issued at Edinburgh in 1761. An elaborate arrangement of the latter, with 12 bars in each part appears in *McGoun's Repository of Scots and Irish Airs, Strathpeys, Reels etc;* published at Glasgow, about 1803.

My Charmer from Clare

Whiteside Mss.

Andante con Sentimente.

48

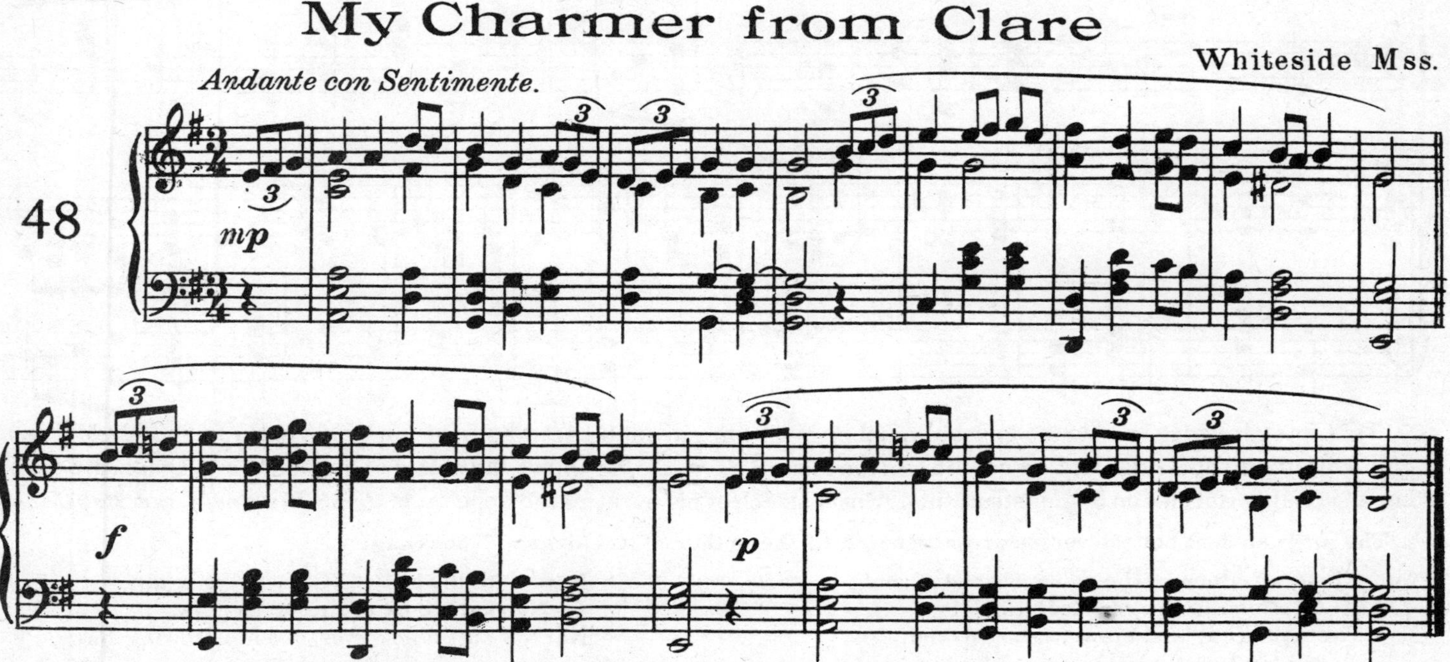

James Whiteside, the "Bard of Bray," County Wicklow was a genius—scholar, poet, musician, composer. Born in County Monaghan in 1844, he retired after 40 years service as schoolteacher at Bray. His playing of the violin won first honors at two Feiseanna. An interesting sketch of his life with likeness, appears on pages 384-7 *Irish Minstrels and Musicians.*

Banished to America.

This fine air which runs to the unusual number of 14 bars in each part was sent me by a Dublin friend Mr. M. Flanagan a distinguished linquist and scholar. In his leisure moments, he enjoys the music of his fiddle, and Union pipes, being a skilful performer on both instruments. A brief sketch of his eventful life appears in ***Irish Minstrels and Musicians***.

The air is ancient but the verses are attributed to the author of the drama "Knocknagow."

Alone, all alone by the wave-washed strand,
All alone in the crowded hall;
The hall is gay, and the waves are grand,
But my heart is not here at all;
It flies far away, by night and by day,
To the times, and the joys that are gone,
And I ne'er can forget, the sweet maiden I met,
In the valley near Sliavnamon!

It was not the grace, of her queenly air,
Nor her cheek of the roses glow,
Nor her soft black eyes, nor her flowing hair,
Nor was it her lily-white brow
'Twas the soul of truth, and of melting ruth,
And the smile like a summer dawn
That stole my heart away, one mild autumn day
In the valley near Sliavnamon.

The Maid of Sweet Gurteen

The song was undoubtedly a best seller among the favorite ballads of a century ago. Probably, stimulated by sympathy for the enamored swain who was forbidden by his proud parent to marry the maid of lower social rating, the song had an amazing run of popularity for a long time.

The setting here presented as noted by Dr. Hudson from the singing of a little girl in the streets of Dublin in 1840 deserves preservation no less than the variants in the Stanford Petrie Collection.

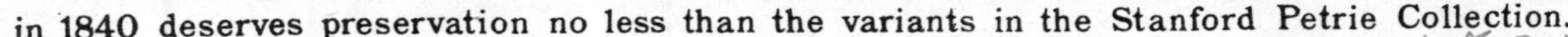

H. Hudson Mss. 1840-41

Ye Banks and Braes o' Bonnie Doon

Wood's Songs of Scotland, Edinburgh, 1848

In the absence of historical evidence, the origin of the air to which this song is set may be open to question. In the correspondence between Robert Burns and his publisher George Thomson, frequent mention is made of the excellence of the Irish airs appropriated for the poet's effusions. From *Wood's Songs of Scotland, Edinburgh, 1848*, edited by Farquhar Graham we quote Burns' own words: "Now to show you how difficult it is to trace the origin of our airs; I have heard it repeatedly asserted that this was an Irish air; nay I have met with an Irish gentleman who affirmed he had heard it in Ireland among the old women; while on the other hand, a countess imformed me that the first person who introduced the air into this country was a baronet's lady of her acquaintance who took down the notes from an itinerant piper in the Isle of Man." Following the above quotation Mr. Graham remarks: "Very recently the publishers met with a sheet song entitled "List! list to my story" published without imprint about 1801, as the water mark on the paper shows, and on which 'Ye Banks and Braes o' Bonnie Doon' is stated to be an Irish air."

O Nancy Wilt Thou Go with Me?

A footnote to this song in *Wood's Songs of Scotland – Edinburgh, 1848* epitomizes its history as follows: "These words by Thomas Percy, Bishop of Dromore, were set to music by Thomas Carter an Irish musician and sung at Vauxhall by Mr. Vernon in 1773, We have inserted this very popular song for the purpose of proclaiming that it belongs to England, tho' a slightly Scotified version of it has been repeatedly published as a Scottish song."

In this ballad the author voices his delight on the release of his wife from appointment as nurse to the infant prince Edward, afterwards Duke of Kent and father of Queen Victoria. Famous as the author of *Reliques of Ancient English Poetry'* Parson Percy was made bishop of Dromore, County of Down, Ireland, where he died in 1811.

Thomas Carter composer of the melody, a native of Dublin studied music under his father Timothy Carter an organist of that city. Under the patronage of the Earl of Inchiquin, he completed his musical education at Naples. He was conductor of a theatre at Bengal, British India, and subsequently at London until his death in 1804.

In review we find that the song above named was written by an Englishman who died in Ireland, and that the music or air to which it is sung was composed by an Irishman who died in England.

Youghal Harbour

Francis E. Walsh. San Francisco

Altho' overlooked by both Bunting and Petrie in their great collections, there can be no question of the antiquity of "Youghal Harbour" which by name and strain is still remembered in the south of Ireland. As a song it was printed in Irish, and under its Irish name *"Eochaill"* in *Hardiman's Irish Minstrelsy, London, 1831,* with the notation; "Few of our national airs are better known than 'Youghal Harbour' which bears a strong resemblance to 'Caithlin Tirriall'. The original words of that favorite rustic ballad have been thought worthy of preservation." About the year 1786 while making the rounds of the Munster circuit, the famous Philpot Curran met an army deserter. The eloquent barrister gave voice to the soldier's feeling in a song entitled "The Deserter"– sometimes called "The Deserter's Meditation"– commencing "If sadly thinking with spirits sinking," which his son and biographer tells us "was adapted to a plaintive Irish air." In No. XVII, of *The Citizen, or Dublin Monthly Magazine* issued in 1841, we find "If Sadly Thinking" in music score with explanatory notes. Again we find it as "Youghal Harbour (If sadly thinking)" without comment in *Haverty's 300 Irish Airs, New York, 1858-9,* differently arranged. In the meantime "Youghal Harbour" had appeared in *Lynch's Melodies of Ireland* an incomplete work issued serially in Dublin, 1845. Among the airs scattered promiscuously in both volumes of *Mooney's History of Ireland, Boston, 1857,* a less florid setting of "Youghal Harbour" in two-four time is to be found. By reason of its rhythm this arrangement was classed with the Hornpipes in the O'Neill Collections.

All works above named being long out of print, and now very rare, it comes within the scope of our aim to supplement the selected version of "Youghal Harbour" printed in Dr. Joyce's last work *Old Irish Folk Music and Song,* by another chosen from four variants submitted by our liberal contributor from California.

In conclusion it may be remarked that while all settings of "Youghal Harbour" preserve a simularity of strain, they may be regarded as essentially different compositions.

The Bard of Armagh

Mary O'Neill

An old-time ballad of the "North Countrie" is "Phelim Brady, the Bard of Armagh," sung to an ancient Irish air, printed for the first time in *O'Neill's Music of Ireland, Chicago, 1903,* as noted down from the singing of his sister by Sergt. James O'Neill. The song in three verses is included in at least two modern compilations.

As this was a dozen years before its appearance in *Herbert Hughs' Collection of Irish Country Songs,* differently arranged, we cannot be accused of trespassing on the musical preserves of others.

This spirited air - included in *Waifs and Strays* by request - tho' not ancient has enjoyed such popularity, that several topical songs have been sung to it. Perhaps its chief merit lies in its availability as a number in a "sett," or quadrille.

Willy Taylor

Do It for My Sake

Wedded to a fine old folk tune, no song enjoyed greater circulation in its day all over Ireland, than "Willy Reilly and His Dear Cuilin Bawn." The adventure commemorated in a ballad of fifteen verses took place not far inland from Donegal Bay, late in the 18th century. The wealthy Squire Folliard's daughter having become enamored of Willy Reilly a handsome stalwart peasant, induced him to elope with her in defiance of the penal laws which endangered his life. The inevitable pursuit was successful, and Reilly was thrown into Sligo Jail, bound hand and foot, and chained to the floor. His fate – freedom or death – depended on the lady's oath. Great was the popular rejoicing when the loyal "Cuilin Bawn" braving her father's anger proclaimed in court:

"The fault is none of Reilly's, the blame is all on me;
I forced him for to leave his place, and come along with me."

As the hero and heroine were of different religious creeds, a certain party spirit excited by the dramatic ballad doubtless increased its popularity. The melody of "Willy Reilly" omitted from the Bunting, and Petrie Collections was included by Dr. Joyce in his last work, *Old Irish Folk Music and Songs,* but in a setting materially different from the above as sung in West Cork in our grandparents' days.

The Bold Trainor O

Capt. F. O'Neill

Moderato

62

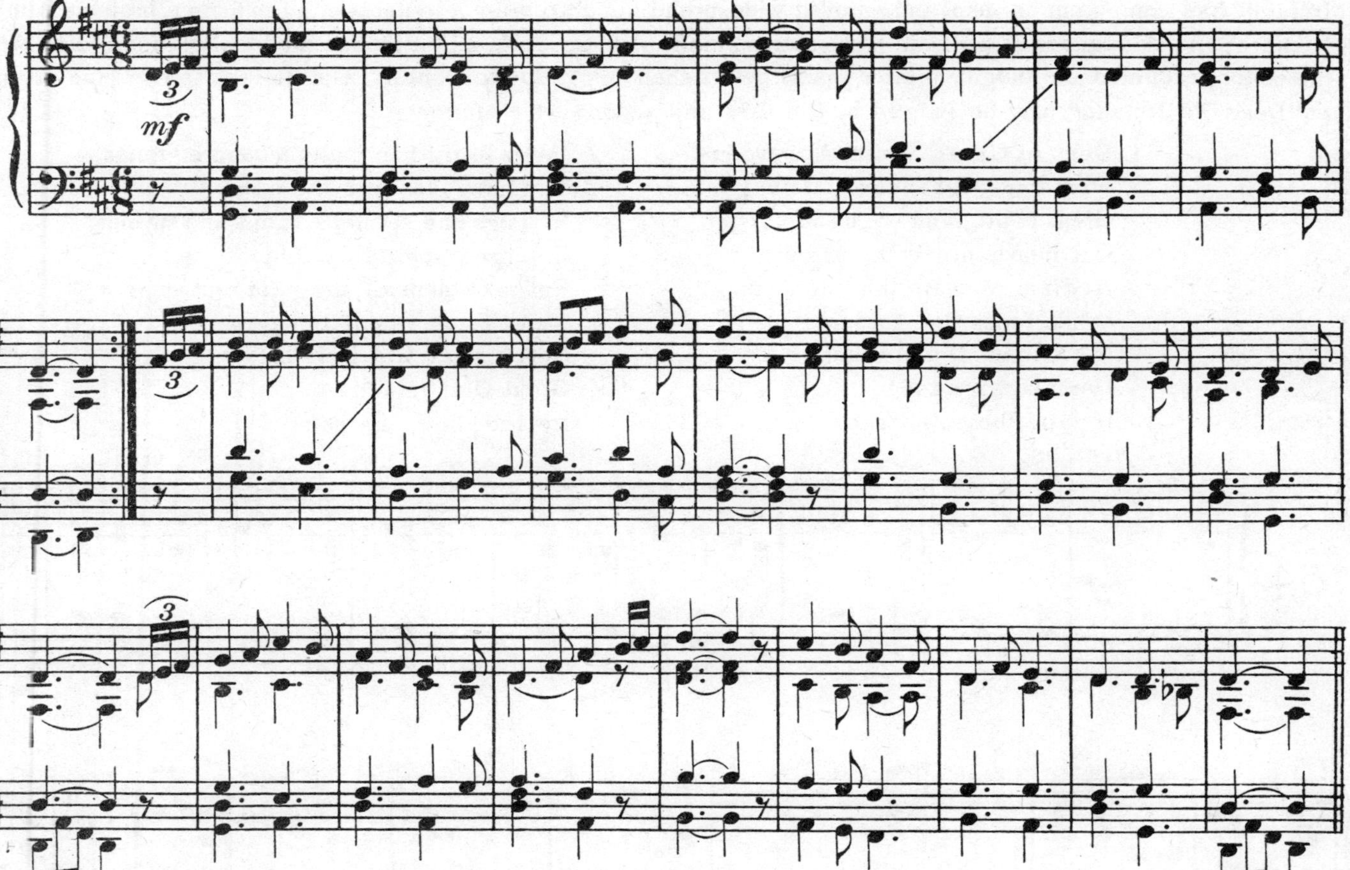

mf

A careful scrutiny of the pages of all available collections of Irish songs or ballads, failed to find any copy of the one-time popular song named as above. The enamored maiden refers to her hero as "My beautiful bold Trainor O," and in voicing her emotions says, "I wrote a petition and sent it to my true love, thinking he might pity on me take." This air which is clearly remembered, I find is suggestive of "The Green Linnet" printed in Dr. Joyce's *Old Irish Folk Music and Songs,* and in the opinion of the editor, compares very favorably with it.

Biddy Magee

Capt. F. O'Neill

From the subconscious memory there revives occasionally a vagrant strain unassociated with any trace of its antecedents. The air of "Biddy Magee" of which song but a few words are remembered, while not ancient, is in the Irish vein, and well worth preserving.

Dear Old Ireland

Capt. F. O'Neill

Long before that rousing ballad "God Save Ireland" was written by T. D. Sullivan, one equally clever "Dear Old Ireland" had come from his pen, and enjoyed widespread popularity for a generation. The famous brothers Timothy D., Richard, and Alexander M. Sullivan were natives of Bantry, Co. Cork, and attended the local National School, (in which the editor graduated and taught in later years) before their migration to Dublin. The defiant spirit of the seven verses of "Dear Old Ireland" may be judged by the first and second which follow:

1. Deep in Canadian woods we've met,
From one bright island flown;
Great is the land we tread but yet
Our hearts are with our own.
And ere we leave this shanty small,
While fades the Autumn day,
We'll toast Old Ireland!
Dear Old Ireland!
Ireland, boys, hurrah!

2. We've heard her faults a hundred times,
The new ones and the old,
In songs and sermons, ranns and rhymes,
Enlarged some fifty fold.
But take them all, the great and small,
And this we've got to say:
Here's dear Old Ireland!
Good Old Ireland!
Ireland, boys, hurrah!

The Heart of My Kitty for Me

H. Hudson Mss. 1840-41

The name favors the classification of this fine old Irish strain as an air, altho its spirit may incline us to believe that if arranged as a double Jig tune it would lose none of its charm. To the "recollection" and singing of Mrs. John Barton; Co. Louth, we are indebted for this melodic gem.

Paddy Will You Now?

Capt. F. O'Neill

66

The above setting differs not materially from that in *Clintons 200 Irish Melodies for the Flute, Dublin, 1840*. Under the same name a much simpler version appears in *Haverty's 300 Irish Airs, New York, 1858,* having but the exceptional number of 13 bars altogether. To the editor this strain was known in boyhood days as "Tow row row" both names being taken from the first line of the song "Tow row row, Paddy will you now" which song by the way cannot be found in any Irish Collection at present available. *"Ta na la"* or "It is day," one of three tunes of that name in the *Stanford-Petrie Collection*, is obviously the same strain. The arrangement however is quite different; the melody and chorus together consisting of but 17 bars.

To add to the diversity, we find that the arrangement of "Paddy Will You Now," to which is set Gavan Duffy's poem "Watch and Wait" in *Ballads and Songs by the Writers of "The Nation" Dublin 1845* is limited to 14 bars.

The Girl I Left Behind Me

Few tunes are more widely known than "The Girl I Left Behind Me," or "The Spalpeen Fanach" as an air, march or hornpipe. Even so, no apology is needed for the introduction of this elaborate setting with variations by Jeremiah Breen, a famous blind fiddler of North Kerry of the past generation. His tunes noted down by a pupil Thomas Rice, were transcribed by a friend Sergt. James P. Walsh of the Chicago Police.

Homeward Bound

Capt. F. O'Neill

68

This spirited march was memorized by the writer in early life; all circumstances relating to its acquirement being now forgotten. We have no assurance of its Gaelic origin, yet few would deny that it was worth preserving at least. For obvious reasons a name has been supplied for its identification.

Lord Lindsay's March

Aird's Selections 1782-97

69

An almost identical setting is named "Capt. Hillman's March" in the same volume.

Over the Hills and Far Away

Capt. F. O'Neill

70

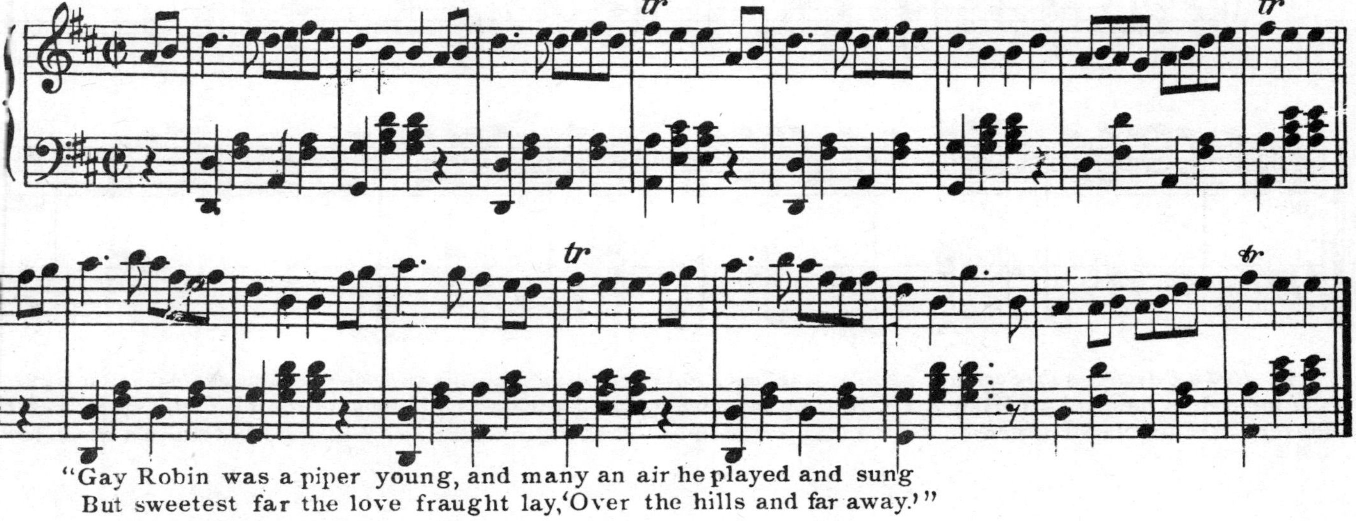

"Gay Robin was a piper young, and many an air he played and sung
But sweetest far the love fraught lay, 'Over the hills and far away.'"

In *Aird's Selections of Scotch, English, Irish and Foreign Airs etc.* this tune is designated "An Irish Jigg" while in the index it is named "An Irish Air". Its emphatic swing and antique cadences, proclaim this spirited strain a march, altho as "The Hibernian Jig" it was included in *O'Neill's Dance Music of Ireland 1907* but in a much lower key.

Bonaparte's Grand March

Sergt. Jas. O'Neill Mss.

74

In the heyday of Bonaparte's renown, early in the nineteenth century, many songs, marches, hornpipes etc. were named in his honor in Ireland. Most of the tunes being traditional still retain their popularity. It is not claimed that "Bonaparte's Grand March" is an Irish composition. In fact we have no information concerning its history or origin, but there can be no question as to its circulation and popularity in Ireland in former times.
Its rescue from the oblivion of faded Mss. to the publicity of the printed page, may endow this spirited march with renewed vitality.

The Croppies' March

"Patsy" Touhey

75

The Croppies' March

(No II.)

Capt. F. O'Neill

76

The term *Croppy* grew from the custom of the English and Scotch reformers in 1795, who cut their hair short. The same custom was adopted by the reformers in Ireland; and hence all those who wore their hair short were denominated *Croppies,* and were the marked objects of government vengeance. In truth, clipped hair constituted secondary evidence of treason, and was sufficient to cause the arrest and ill treatment of any person daring enough to adopt it.

Port Gordon

O'Farrell's Pocket Companion 1804-10

77

In *Hardiman's Irish Minstrelsy, Vol. I.* "Port Gordon" is listed as one of Carolan's compositions, and it is also attributed to him in *O'Farrell's Pocket Companion for the Irish or Union Pipes,* from which the above setting was copied. Bunting however includes "Port Gordon" among the compositions of Rory Dall O'Cahan a famous harper of the Western Highlands. The fact is that Carolan exercised his talents in retouching his predecessor's composition according to his own personal fancy.

The setting which follows taken from *O'Neill's Music of Ireland* was found among Sergt. James O'Neill's inherited Mss.

Gordon's Tune

Sergt. Jas. O'Neill

78

Long John's Wedding March

Capt. F. O'Neill

79

The foregoing march is an elaboration of a Jig named "Long John's Wedding" No. 233, *O'Neill's Dance Music of Ireland.*

Slash Away the Pressing Gang

Capt. F. O'Neill

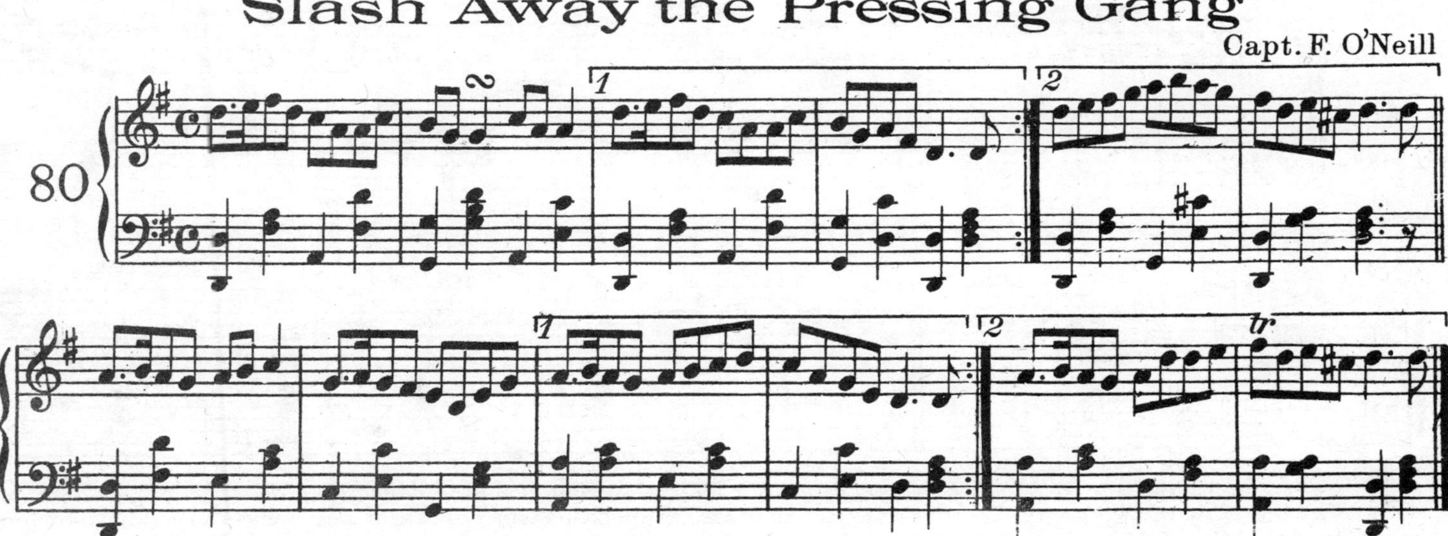

Dalkeith Maiden

Aird's Selections 1782-97

81

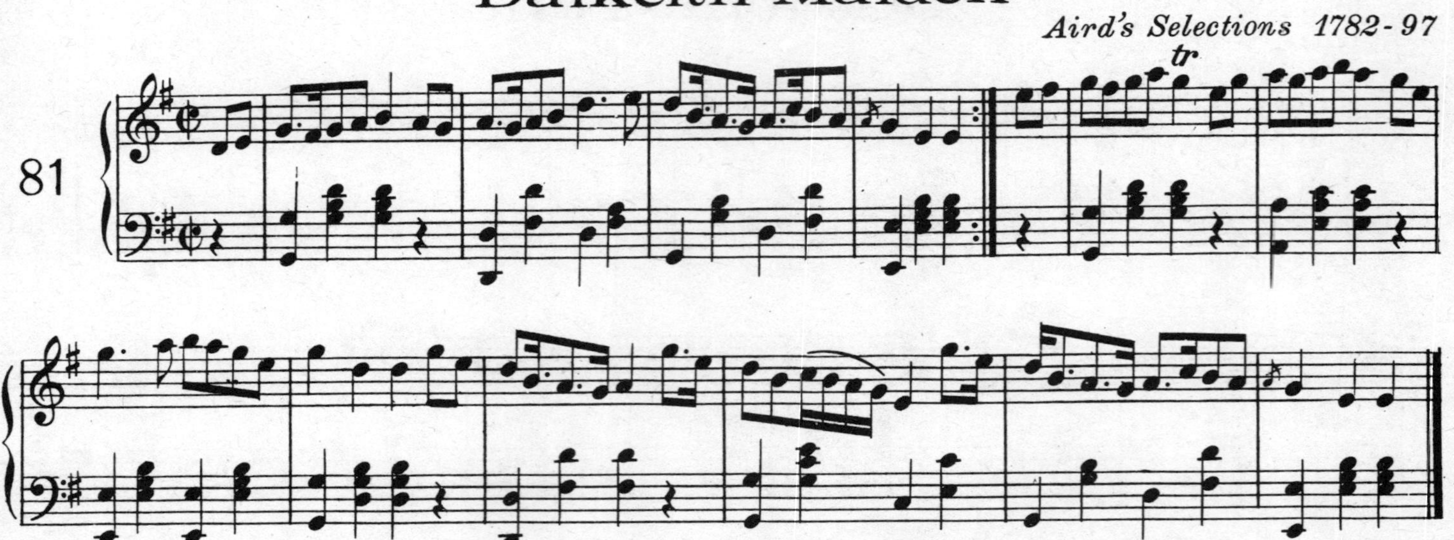

There is enough resemblance between the above melody and that which follows, to suggest a common origin. The "Dalkeith Maiden" was taken from *Aird's Selection of Scotch, English, Irish and Foreign Airs, Vol. III,* published in Glasgow, 1788. The earliest setting of "Biddy I'm not Jesting" available is that obtained by Petrie in 1829 from Paddy Coneely the famous Galway piper, and which appears in the key of A flat in the *Stanford Petrie Colletion of Irish Music.* The source of this memorized version of earlier years, cannot now be recalled by the writer.

Biddy I'm Not Jesting

Capt. F. O'Neill

82

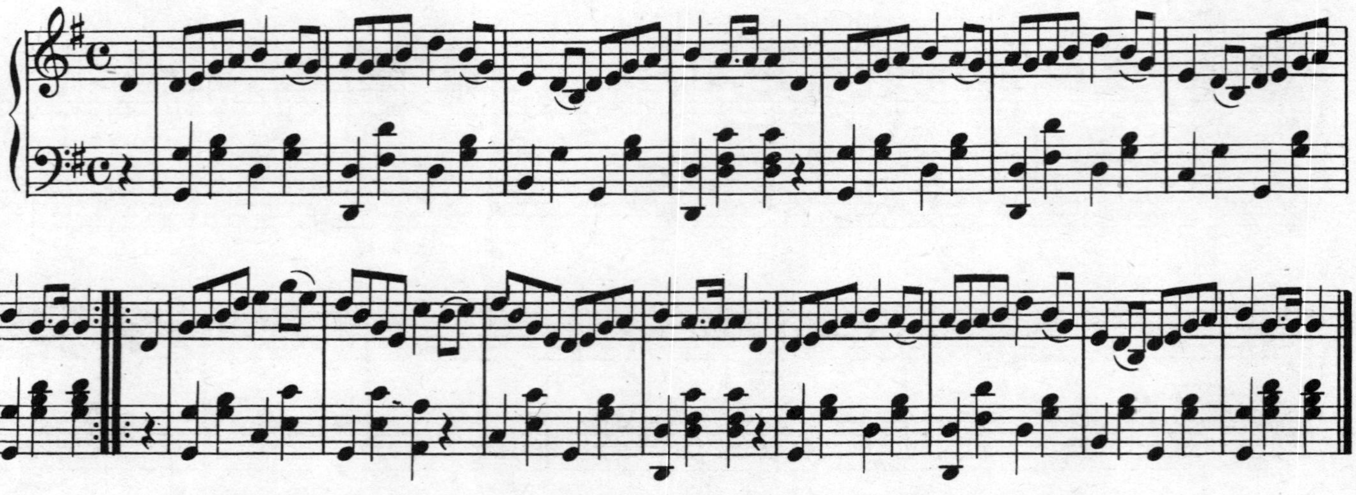

The Gobby O and Variations*

Rice-Walsh Mss.

83

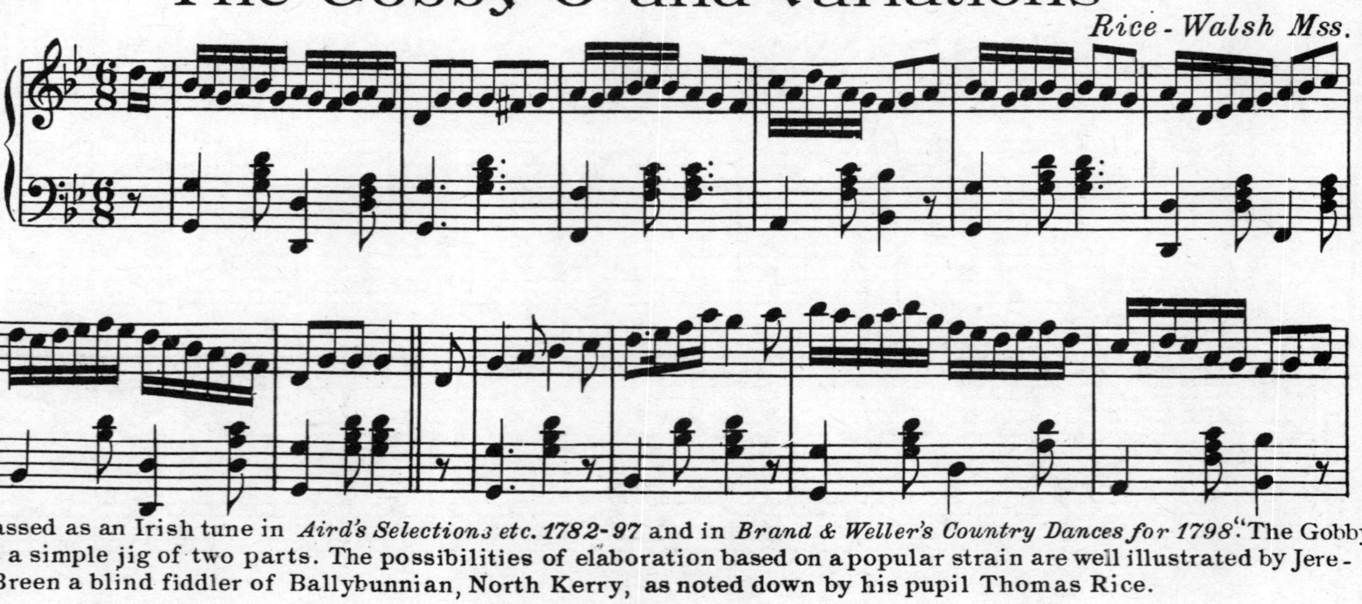

* Classed as an Irish tune in *Aird's Selections etc. 1782-97* and in *Brand & Weller's Country Dances for 1798.* "The Gobby O" was a simple jig of two parts. The possibilities of elaboration based on a popular strain are well illustrated by Jeremiah Breen a blind fiddler of Ballybunnian, North Kerry, as noted down by his pupil Thomas Rice.

THE GOBBY O & VARIATIONS (Con.)

Johnny I Hardly Knew Ye

Capt. F. O'Neill

84

Classed as a street ballad in *Halliday Sparling's Irish Minstrelsy London 1887* the editor adds in a note page 366. "Johnny I Hardly knew ye! This favorite old song is here for the first time given complete. It dates from the beginning of the present century,(19th) when Irish regiments were so extensively raised for the East India Service."
This spirited air almost forgotten in Ireland blossomed into new popularity during the American civil war, and after its arrangement by a master hand–Patrick Sarsfield Gilmore– it became a great favorite with military and volunteer bands. Parodies on the original song such as "When Johnny Comes Marching Home Again," "Johnny Fill Up the Bowl" etc. were sung to it by the Union soldiers. After the manner of the *Loobeens* and occupational songs of olden days in Ireland, additional verses were improvised, some possibly crude, yet always mirth - provoking, and well calculated to keep up their spirits on the march, or relieve the monotony of camp life.
The circumstance of its arrangement as above stated no doubt led Adair Fitz Gerald to refer to it in his *Stories of Famous Songs* in qualified words, "When Johnny Comes Marching Home Again" said to have been composed by the celebrated Patrick S. Gilmore." The latter a native of Dublin, quite probably had memorized the tune in his youth. The original, it may be observed, included a refrain of four lines not found in the parodies.

The Bonnie Blue Flag

Capt. F. O'Neill

85

Not less popular than the preceding in the north, was "The Bonnie Blue Flag," the Southern National Air, which was to the boys in grey what "Yankee Doodle" was to the boys in blue. In Adair Fitz Gerald's *Famous songs* we are told the words of "The Bonnie Blue Flag" were written in 1862 by Mrs Annie Chambers Ketchum to an Irish melody adapted or composed by Henry McCarthy. After a fruitless search in several old time collections for the now very rare strain it is presented as noted from the editor's memory.

Dandy Pat

Capt. F. O'Neill

This spirited air enjoyed no little popularity some fifty years ago when a song of that name to be found in *Hyland's Mammoth Hibernian Songster* was sung to it.

McDermot Roe

Carolan - Hibernian Muse, 1787

87

Among Carolan's many distinguished friends and patrons, no one was more generous and loyal than Mrs. McDermot Roe, of Alderford House, County Roscommon. At the outset of his professional career in 1693, it was she who equipped him with a horse and an attendant harper; and it was to her hospitable home he directed his feeble footsteps in his declining days. Exceptionally honored in death, Carolan's remains were interred near the family vault of his benefactress.

Miss Forbes' Return

Sergt. Jas. O'Neill, Mss.

88

"Miss Forbes' Return" as noted by Humphrey Murphy in Sergt. O'Neill's Mss. differs not materially from "Miss Forbes Farewell" as printed in *Aird's Selections of Scotch, English, Irish and Foreign Airs 1782-97.* This strain is no less popular in Ireland than it is with Highland pipers everywhere. It may be claimed that Murphy's variant is more Irish in character than the original.

Pat on Parade

Capt. F. O'Neill

89

This March or Hornpipe tune noted from memory may be worthy of preservation, but when or where it was acquired the writer is unable to state. Suggestion supplied the name.

Moonlight on the Lough

Rice-Walsh Mss

90

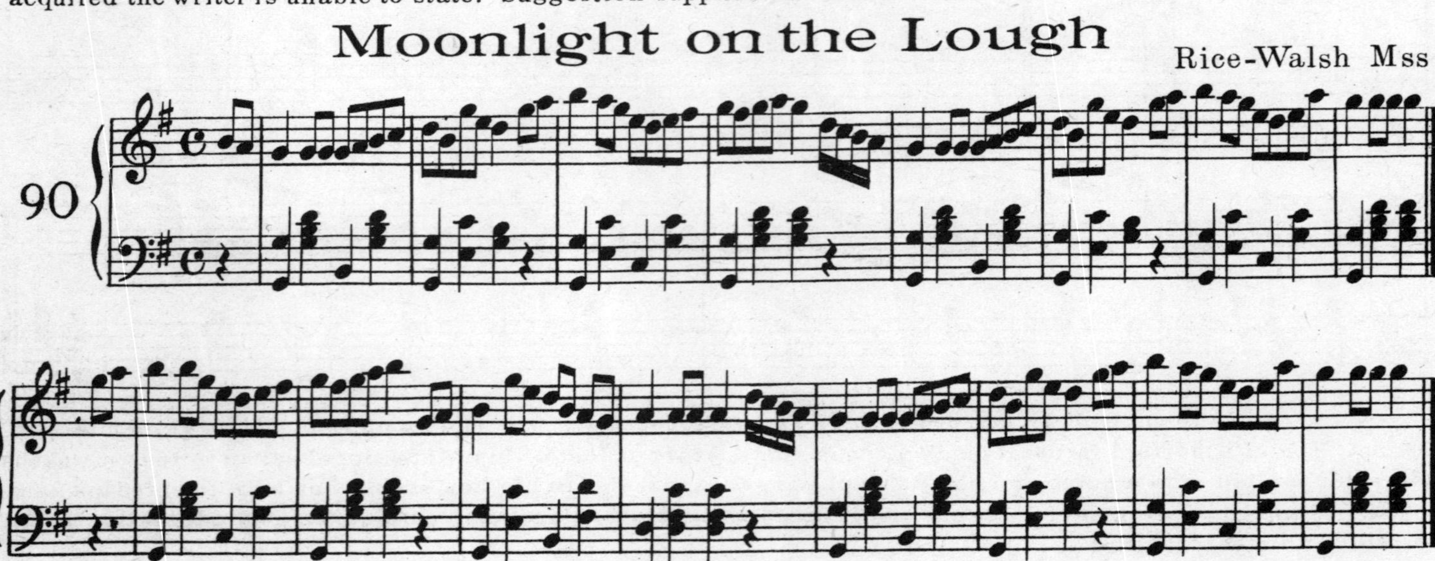

The marching tune which follows was another of McLean's favorites, which seems to be unknown to the pipers of this generation. The original name not being ascertained, a suggested title is here presented. McLean was a native of Ross, Scotland.

The above fine marching tune tho' manifestly in the Irish style is probably of Scotch origin because it comes from the subconscious memory of the writer who associated in Chicago nearly fifty years ago, with such noted Highland pipers as McLean, Cant, and Monroe.

Of the four distinct tunes, named after Lochiel the Jacobite hero to be found in old printed Collections, I find that one specially arranged for the Highland bagpipe is a variant of "Johnny's Trip to France", dreamily remembered by the editor since early manhood.

O'Sullivan's March

Rice - Walsh Mss.

93

The above is an involved variant of a much simpler jig tune of identical name printed in *Lynch's Melodies of Ireland 1845*; and in *O'Neill's Dance Music of Ireland 1907*. The strain is ancient. Following is a quatrain of a folk song sung to it in the editor's boyhood days.

"There was an old woman tossed up in a blanket
Seventeen times as high as the moon:
What she was doing there I cannot imagine
But in her hand she carried a broom."

All of which is reminiscent of the days of witchcraft.

Gladly Would I Go

Capt. F. O'Neill

This fine old march was memorized from the playing of William McLean a famous Highland piper much admired in Chicago some fifty years ago. The tune in almost identical setting was included in a book of pipe music, published at Glasgow about 1825 under two names: "The Duke of Athol's March" and a long Gaelic title expressive of romance and chivalry. Its spirited swing and characteristic cadences, no less than its Gaelic title indicate an Irish origin.

No Surrender

H. Hudson Mss. 1840-41

The setting of "No Surrender" above submitted, was taken from a manuscript volume of Irish melodies compiled by H. Hudson 24 Stephen's Green, Dublin in the years 1840-41. After the name comes the notation "From Ordnance Survey of Londonderry, vol. 1, page 197." From the remarks accompanying the famous old march in *Dr. Joyce's Ancient Irish Music Dublin, 1890*, we quote: "It is printed in the Ordnance Memoir of Londondery, where however it is practically inaccessible to the general public, as that book is very scarce. It has long been appropriated as the marching tune of the yearly celebration of the shutting and opening of the gates of Derry." It may be of interest to add that the seige of Derry occurred in 1689.

We may be pardoned for remarking that Dr. Joyce's arrangment is in the Scale of C altho both settings were derived from the same scarce publication.

The Knight of St. Patrick Lancers

Sergt Jas. O'Neill, Mss.

96

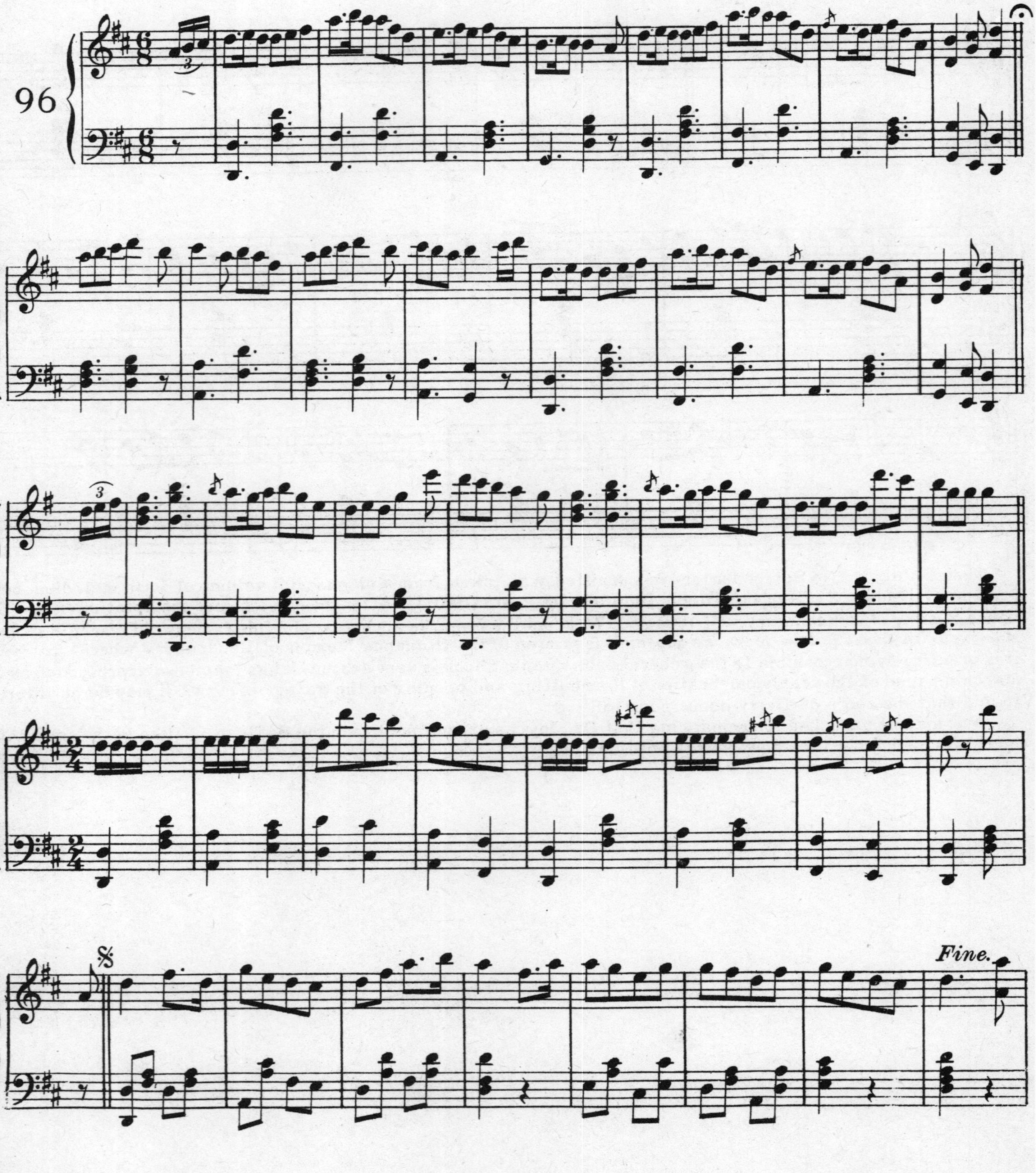

Fine.

The Knight of St. Patrick Lancers (con.)

The Knight of St. Patrick Lancers (con.)

D.S.

The Knight of St. Patrick Lancers (con.)

The Knight of St. Patrick Lancers (con.)

The Knight of St. Patrick Lancers (con.)

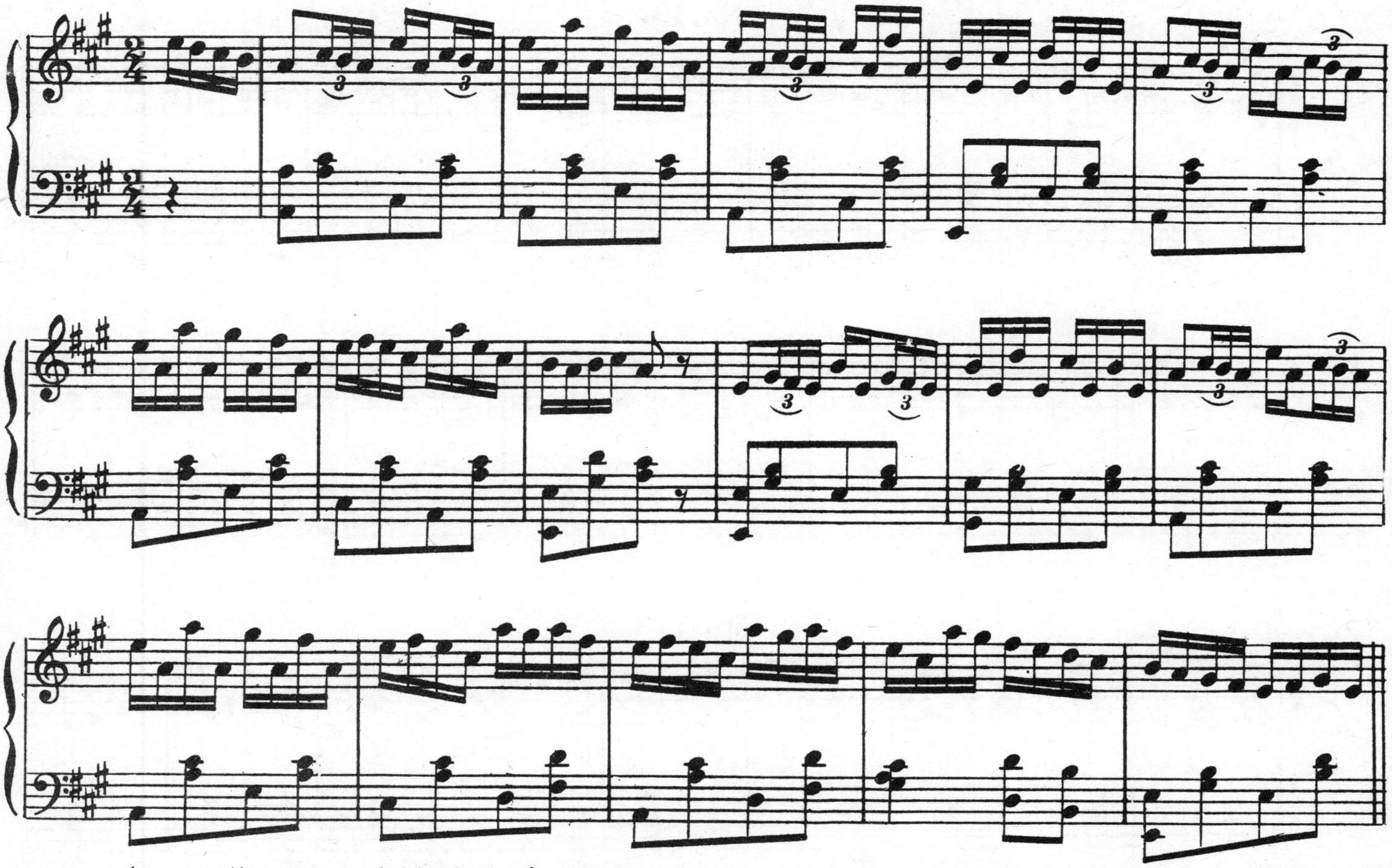

Among the mass of his father's manuscript music which Sergt. James O'Neill brought from Belfast in his youth, was a copy of "The Knight of St. Patrick Lancers." Many of the original tunes of which it was composed having been subjected to alteration in the process of arrangement, its publication in that form in the O'Neill Collections was then not favorably considered. Since the appearance of Dr. Joyce's *Old Irish Folk Music and Songs* in 1909 the composition has assumed new interest. In a note to a "Reel," page 63, the learned author remarks: "I find a setting different from mine in a single obscure publication *The Knight of St. Patrick Lancers*, long since out of print." Dr. Joyce's unnamed "Reel" it may be added is the well known "Bonnie Kate." Taking all things into consideration *The Knight of St. Patrick Lancers*, cannot be out of place in a collection of *Waifs and Strays of Gaelic Melody*.

Winter Garden Quadrille

No. I

Sergt Jas. O'Neill, Mss.

97

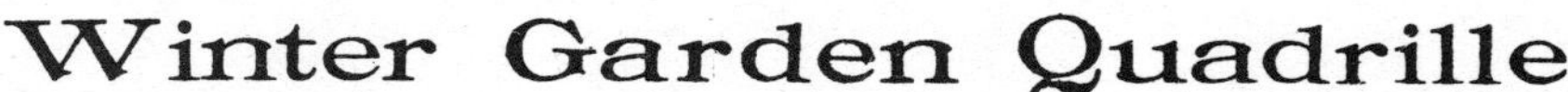

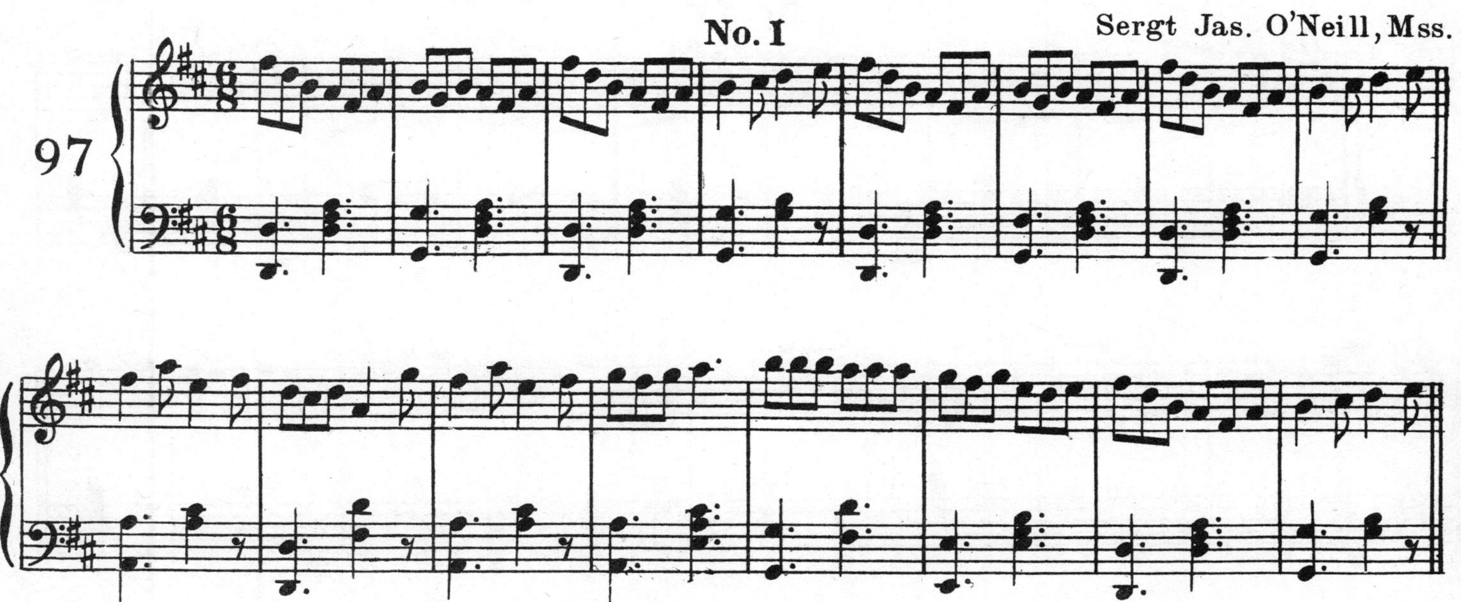

Winter Garden Quadrille (con.)

No. III

No. IV

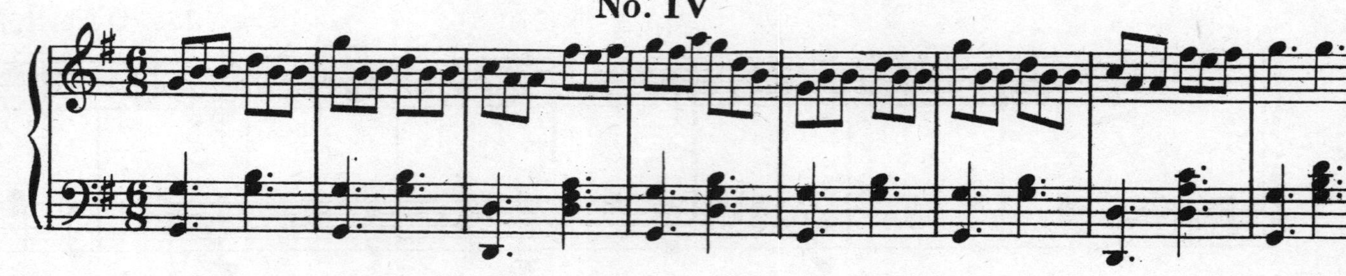

The following spirited tune was found among the O'Neill M.S.S., but without a title— With a view to its identification in the Index we have named it

This is a variant of the Long Dance of the same name in *O'Neill's Dance Music of Ireland*. It differs however in having two bars less in the second part.

The Humors of Listivain

Aird's Selections 1782-97

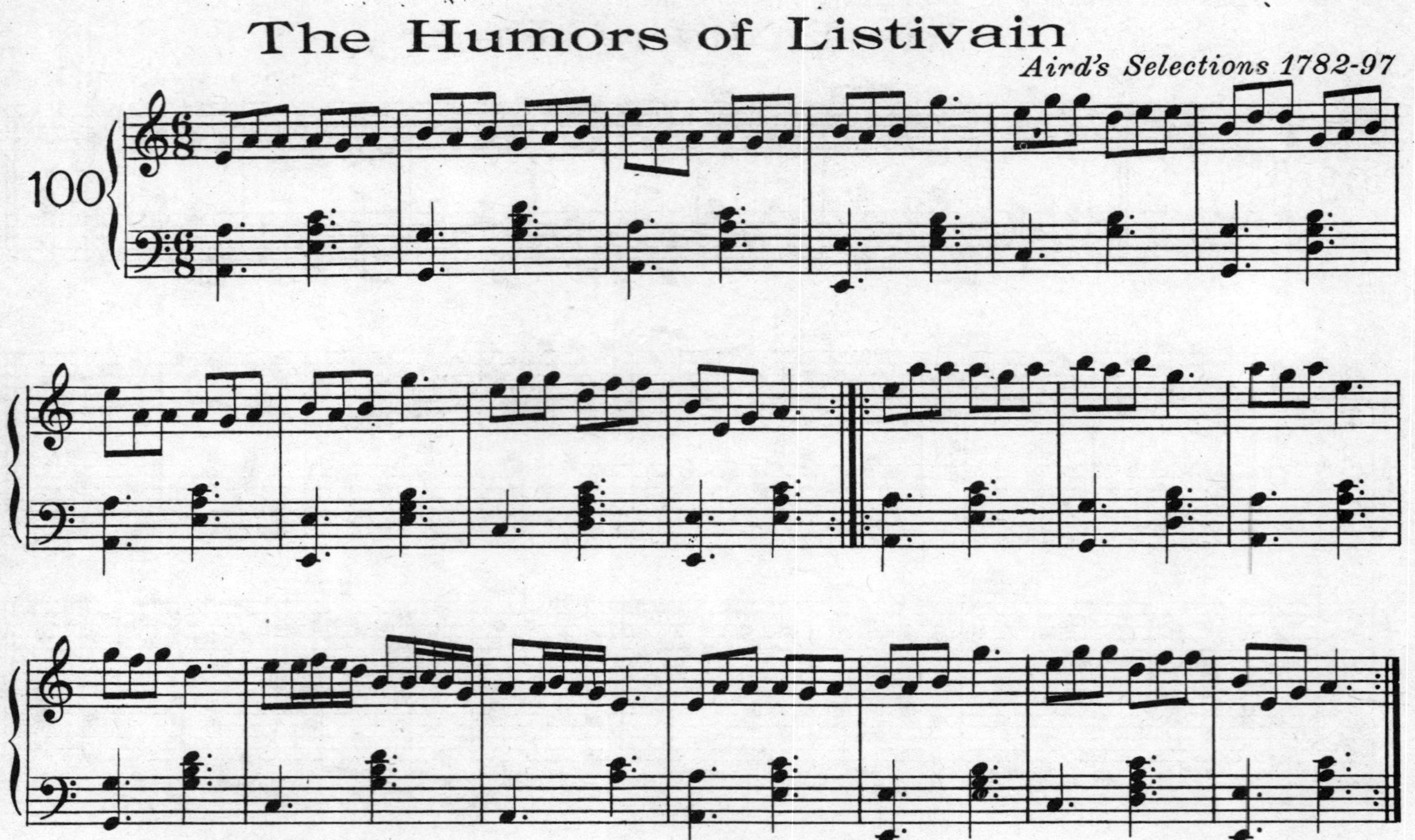

The above setting of which there are several variants, is no doubt the original. In *O Farrell's National Irish Music for the Union Pipes, 1797-1800,* a tune named "Jerry's Rambles" closely follows it. More distinct variants are "The Jolly Old Woman," and "The Humors of Bandon," the latter as printed in *O'Neill's Dance Music of Ireland* being the arrangement favored by modern dancers.

Morgiana in Ireland

O'Farrell's Pocket Companion 1804-10

Suisin Ban, or White Blanket
(Old Style)
O'Farrell's Pocket Companion 1804-10
102
The Cruiskin
Sergt. Jas. O'Neill, Mss.
103
Walsh's Frolics
Francis E. Walsh,
San Francisco
104
tr

An identical setting with variations was printed in *Burk Thumoth's Twelve English, and Twelve Irish Airs, London 1743.*

Hibernian Dance
Clinton's Irish Melodies 1840
108
The Wild Irishman
The Hibernian Muse 1787
109
Tom Jones
(Irish)
Aird's Selections 1782-97
110

Merrily Kissed the Quaker

For over a century the above name has been associated with a tune or Special Dance in Ireland, but no song or verse relating thereto has been traced. In *O'Farrell's Pocket Companion for the Irish or Union Pipes 1804-10,* we find the tune with name annotated "New Sett Irish". Continuing the investigation we discover that "Merrily Dance the Quaker" (probably the original tune) was printed in No.7 of *Bremner's Collection of Scots Reels, or Country Dances* issued in 1760. The traditional version in North Kerry taken from the Rice-Walsh Mss. serves to illustrate how far a tune may deviate from the original in a few generations.

Rosin the Bow

Serg't. Jas. O'Neill Mss.

The name "Rosin the Bow" has clung to the writer's memory since childhood, and the tune like the song about "Old Rosin the Bow" (a nickname for the fiddler) may have passed into oblivion, had not the melody been fortuitously found recently in a faded miscellaneous Mss. Collection long discarded by Sergt. James O'Neill. A version of it I find is printed in *Joyce's Old Irish Folk Music and Songs - 1909*.

Tulloch Gorm

Supplied by Off. William Walsh

115

Sometimes written "Tulloch Gorum" or "Tullagorum", this famous strathspey first published in *Rob't Bremner's Collection of Scots Reels or Country Dances, Edinburgh 1757* was composed by William Marshall, butler and house stewart in the service of the Duke of Gordon for thirty years. His tunes were plagiarized ruthlessly by contemporaries. In the words of Robert Burns, Marshall was "the first composer of strathspeys in the age" - The grace notes peculiar to pipe music are omitted in this setting. A clergyman at Linshart, Rev. John Skinner composed songs to "Tulloch Gorum" and several others of Marshall's tunes.

The Reel of Tulloch

Neil Gow & Sons Complete Repository c, 1805

116

Noted for its dashing rhythm rather than for its melodic merits "The Reel of Tulloch" first appeared in print in the 10th number of *Robert Bremner's Scots Reels or Country Dances* issued in 1761. It originated in the parish of Tulloch, Aberdeenshire, Scotland. The traditional stories relating to its composition are too long and unreliable for narration here. A wild orgie of dancing under improbable circumstances in one case, and a desperate encounter with swords in another, are given as the inspiration of what has been termed "the maddest of all Highland reels." Altho officer William Walsh obligingly favored me with a bagpipe setting of the tune, preference has been given to that played by the famous violinist Neil Gow, which leaves nothing to be desired.

Gillie Callum - Sword Dance

Known also as, Keellum Kallum

Supplied by Off. William Walsh, Chicago

117

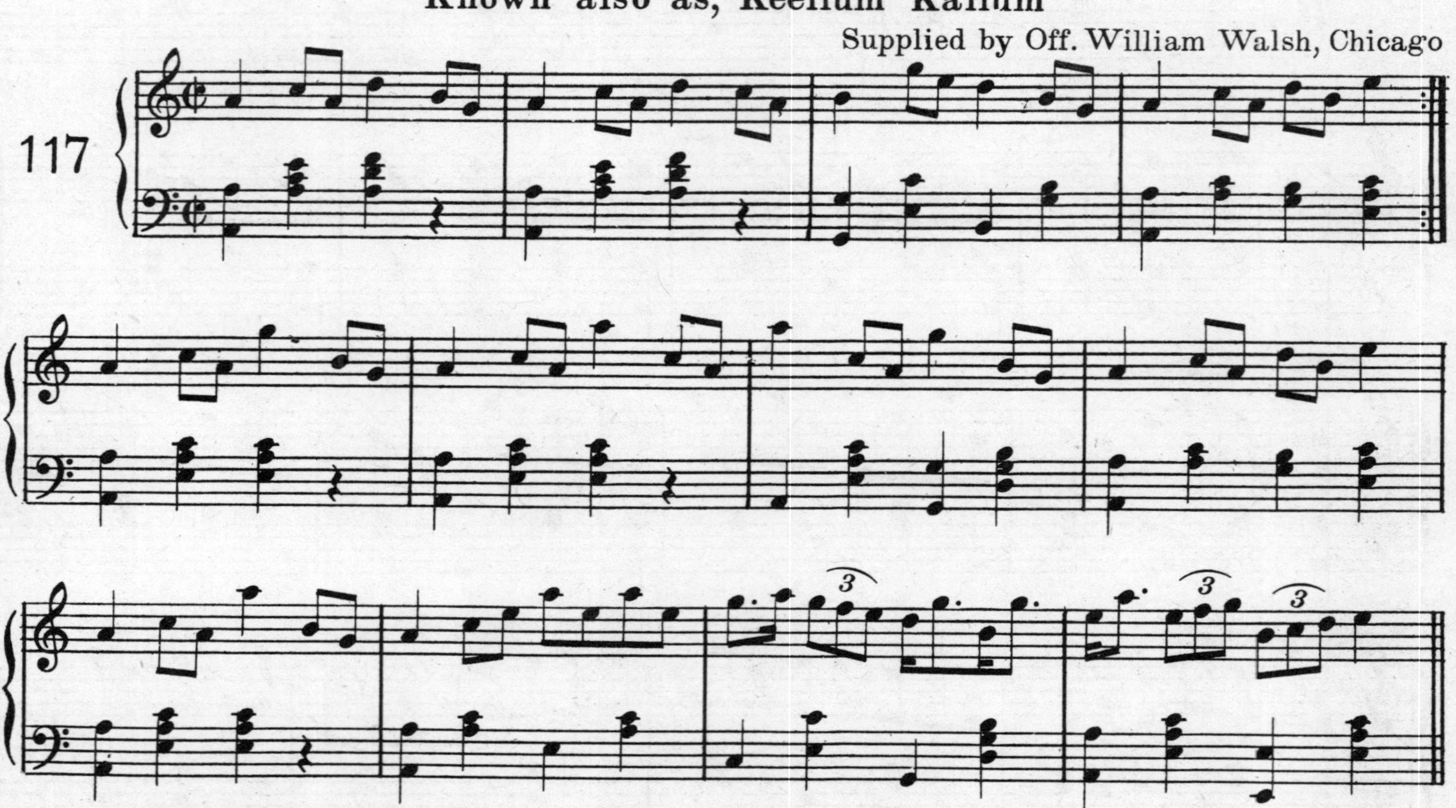

This characteristic Scottish dance tune, was first printed in *Bremner's 2d Collection of Scots Reels or Country Dances, London 1768*. Like most tunes of that early date, the composer's name is unknown. The origin of the name is traced to *Callum a chinn mhoir*, anglicised Malcolm Canmore, which signifies Callum of the big head. He incurred the displeasure of the Highlanders by marrying a Saxon princess which involved many unpopular changes. Gillie Callum, or Callum's tax-gatherer (an odious official everywhere) has been immortalized in melody, while the traditional story is well nigh forgotten.

The Sword Dance is of high antiquity, and diversified in form according to race, and the period of its practice. The picturesque Sword Dance of the agile Highlanders alone, has survived to the present day.

Shaun Truish Willichan

Preston's Reprint of Bremner's Collections London 1789

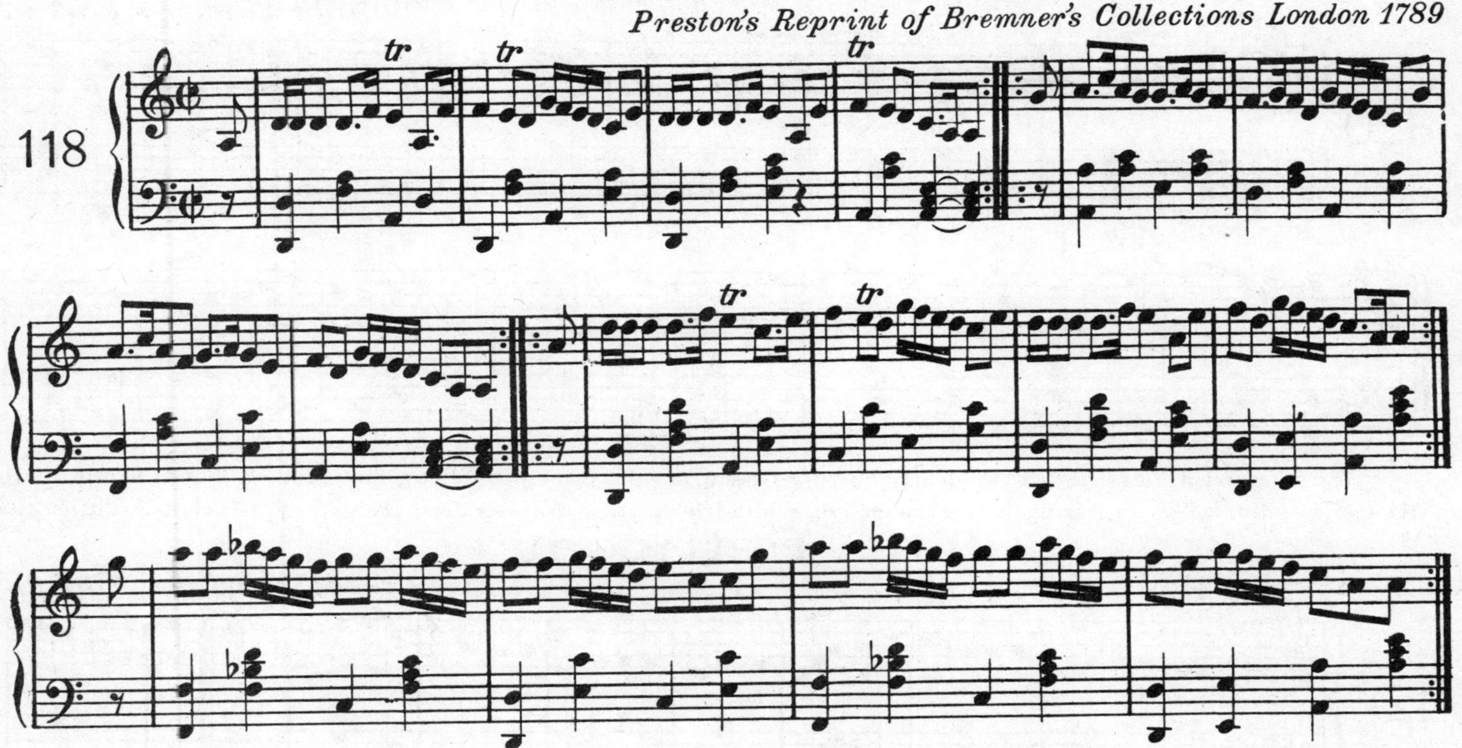

With this tune is associated a special Highland dance, commonly referred to as "Sean Truis," but occasionally as "Willichan" The full name as above given is the same in Glen's Analytical Table, and in *Bremner's Collections of Scots Reels, or Country Dances 1757-61*. After Robert Bremner's death in 1789 his Collections were reprinted by Preston, a great London publisher.

Whistle o'er the Leave o't

The Caledonian Muse 1785

Identical with the above setting of "Whistle o'er the Leave o't" is that printed in *Bremner's Collection of Scots Reels or Country Dances–1757-61*. Its claim to consideration in this work is based on the statement of Joseph Cant of Chicago, a first prize winner at several piping competitions; that it was the favorite tune for the *Sean Truis* or "Old Man's Dance" in his native Perthshire. The rhythm of it was deemed more suitable to the requirements of dancers burdened with years than the preceding tune. On such excellent authority it has been included in this classification.

Ligrum Cus

(Irish)

Aird's Selections 1782-97

The expression "*Ligrum Cus*" evidently corrupt Gaelic, may be translated "Let go my foot". It may also relate to the rent question. We can hardly blame the Scotch, while Irish titles in ***Moore's Irish Melodies*** present similar difficulties.

The Petticoat

Aird's Selections 1782-97

121

Paddy Stack's Fling

Patrick Stack, Chicago

122

Bonny Woods and Braes

Capt. F. O'Neill

123

Known only as "The Highland Fling" this cheerful tune has served for that purpose as long as the editor can remember. For its name as above printed, we are indebted to Offr. William Walsh whose memory in such matters is phenomenal. The original however was "The Marquis of Hastings' Strathspey."

The Lark in the Morning

James Carbray
(Quebec Canada)

124

Mr. Carbray now of Chicago, a versatile musician himself learned "The Lark in the Morning" from a Kerry fiddler named Courtney. It is an old time Set Dance of marked rhythm and originality, and was first printed in *O'Neills Music of Ireland, Chicago, 1902*

Wink and I'll Follow You

(Single Jig)

Capt. F. O'Neill

125

The Single Jig, like the Double Jig is in six eight time, but differs from the latter chiefly in having at most but one triplet in each bar. More ancient than the Double Jig, the dance steps of the Single Jig are more light and graceful.

Double Jigs

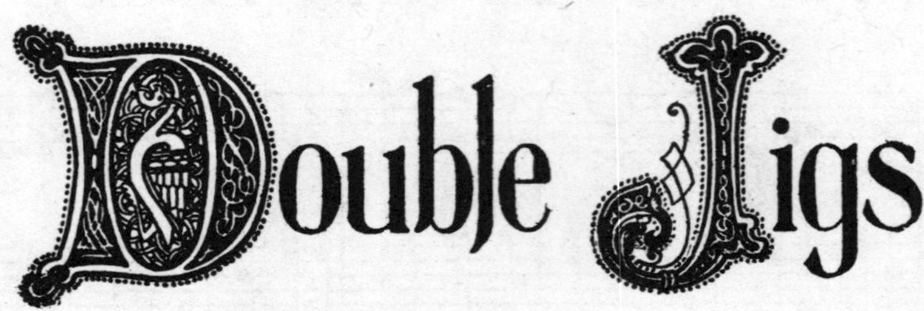

The Humors of Ross

O'Farrell's Pocket Companion 1804-10

126

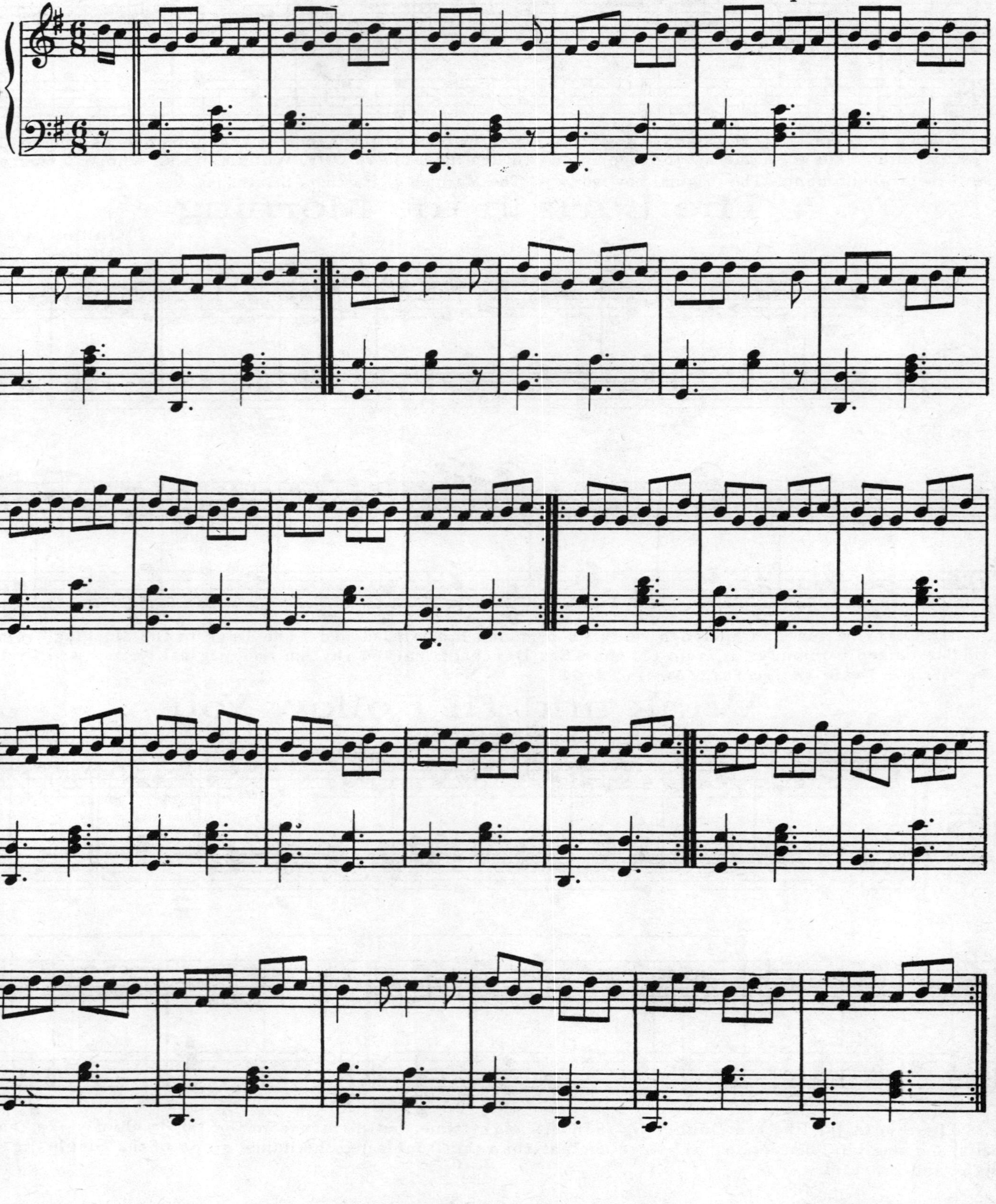

The Sporting Irishman
Clinton's Irish Melodies 1840
127
A Boy from Home
Patrick Stack - Chicago.
128
The Girl that Wears Green
Sergt. Jas. O'Neill Mss.
129

Bantry Bay Boys
Riley's Country Dances for 1798
130
A Trip to Killarney
O'Farrell's Pocket Companion 1804-10
131

Melvin Head

Sergt. Jas. O'Neill Mss.

132

Jerry O'Reilly's, Jig

Jeremiah O'Reilly, San Francisco, Cal.

133

Paddy the Weaver

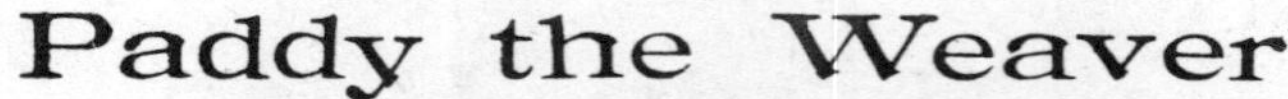

Wilson's Companion to the Ballroom. 1816

134

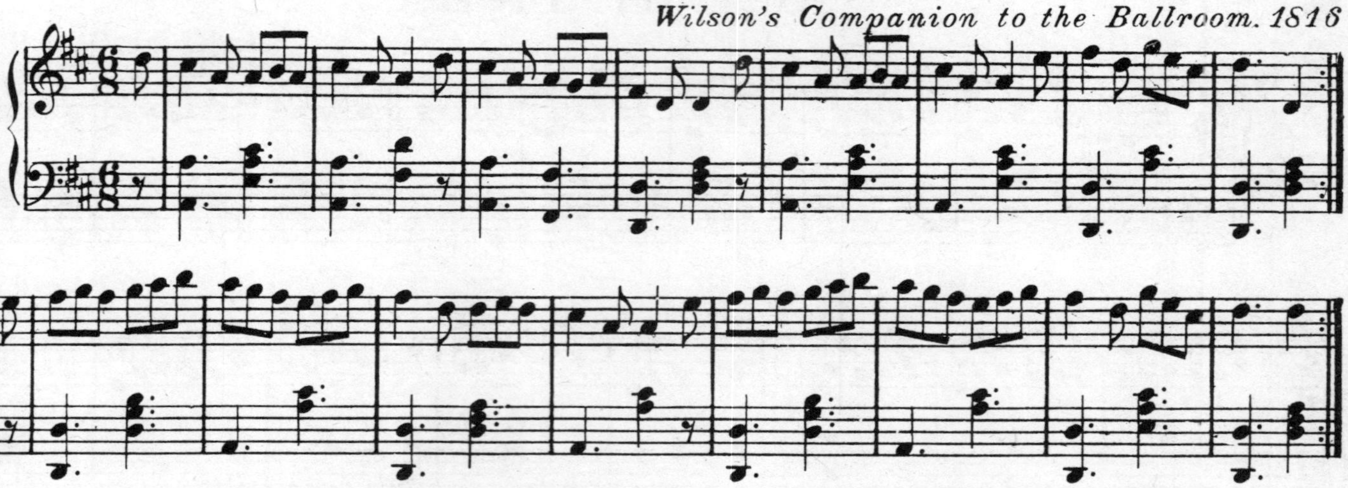

Original Old Horned Sheep

Capt. F. O'Neill

135

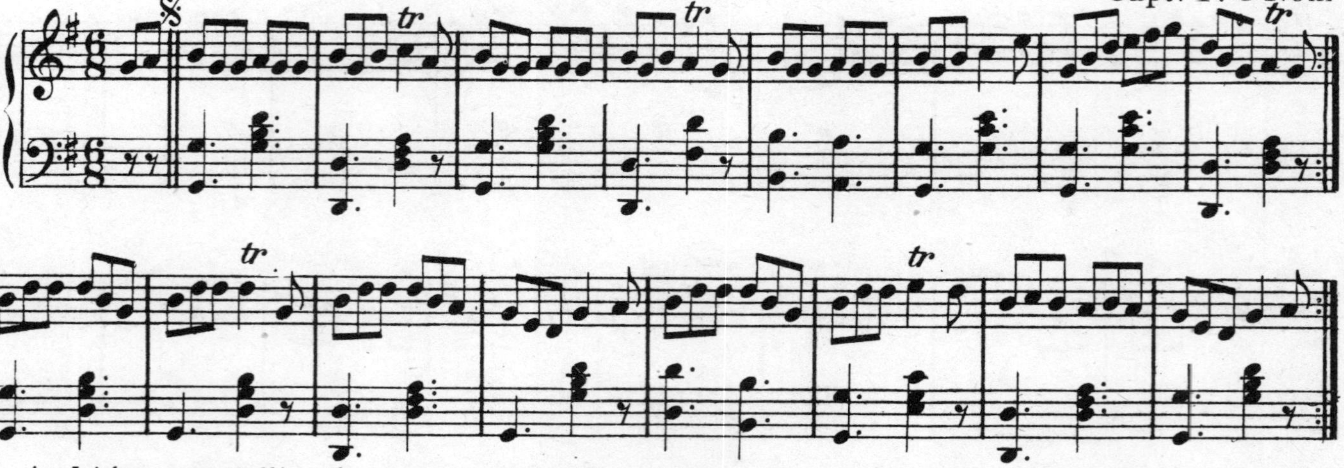

An Irish song extolling the many good, qualities of *"an sean caora adarcach"* in supplying drink, food, and clothing, to her owner, was sung to this air. No. 238 in *O'Neill's Dance Music of Ireland* is a sprightly variant.

Oxford Castle

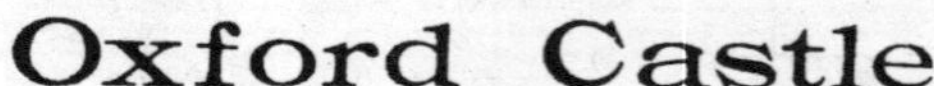

Aird's Selections 1782-97.

136

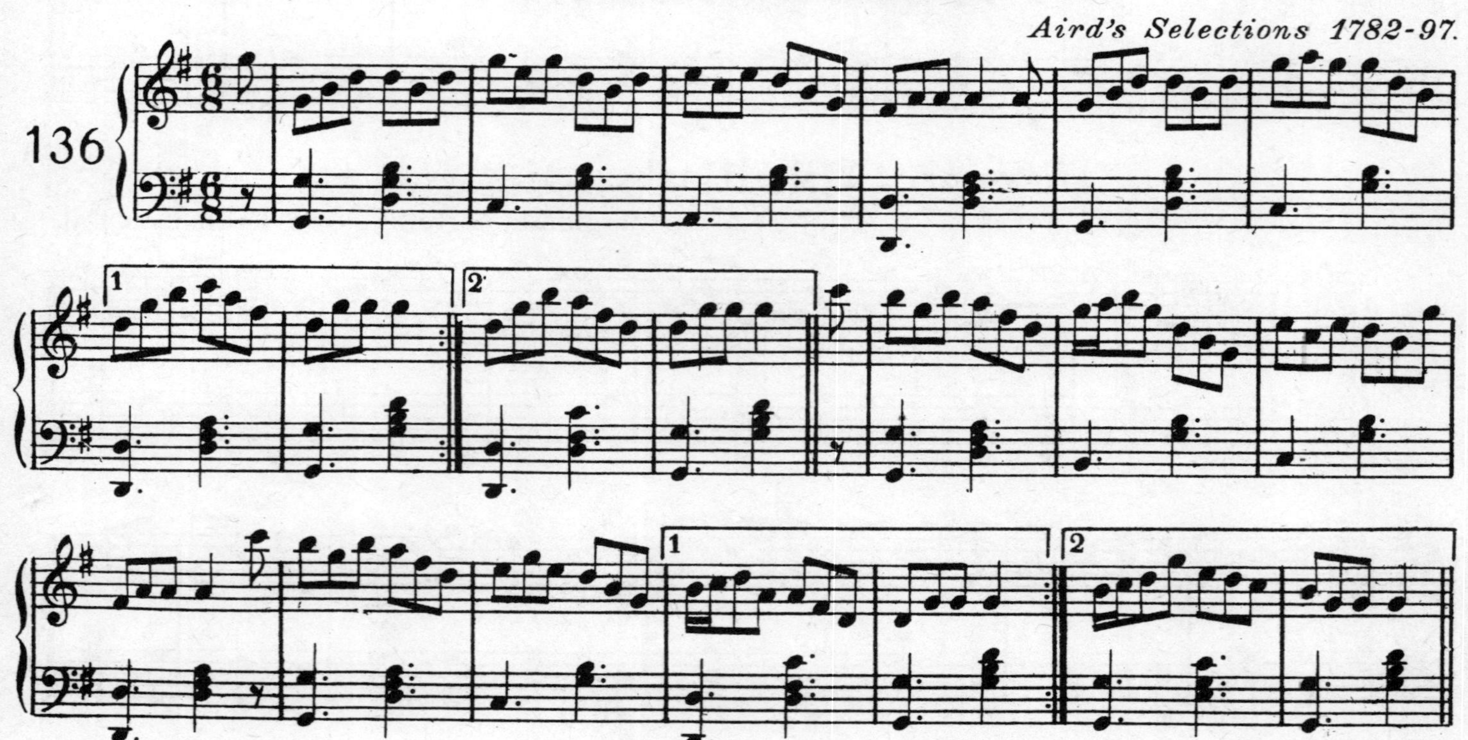

Give Me a Lass with a Lump of Land

Aird's Selections, 1782-97.

137

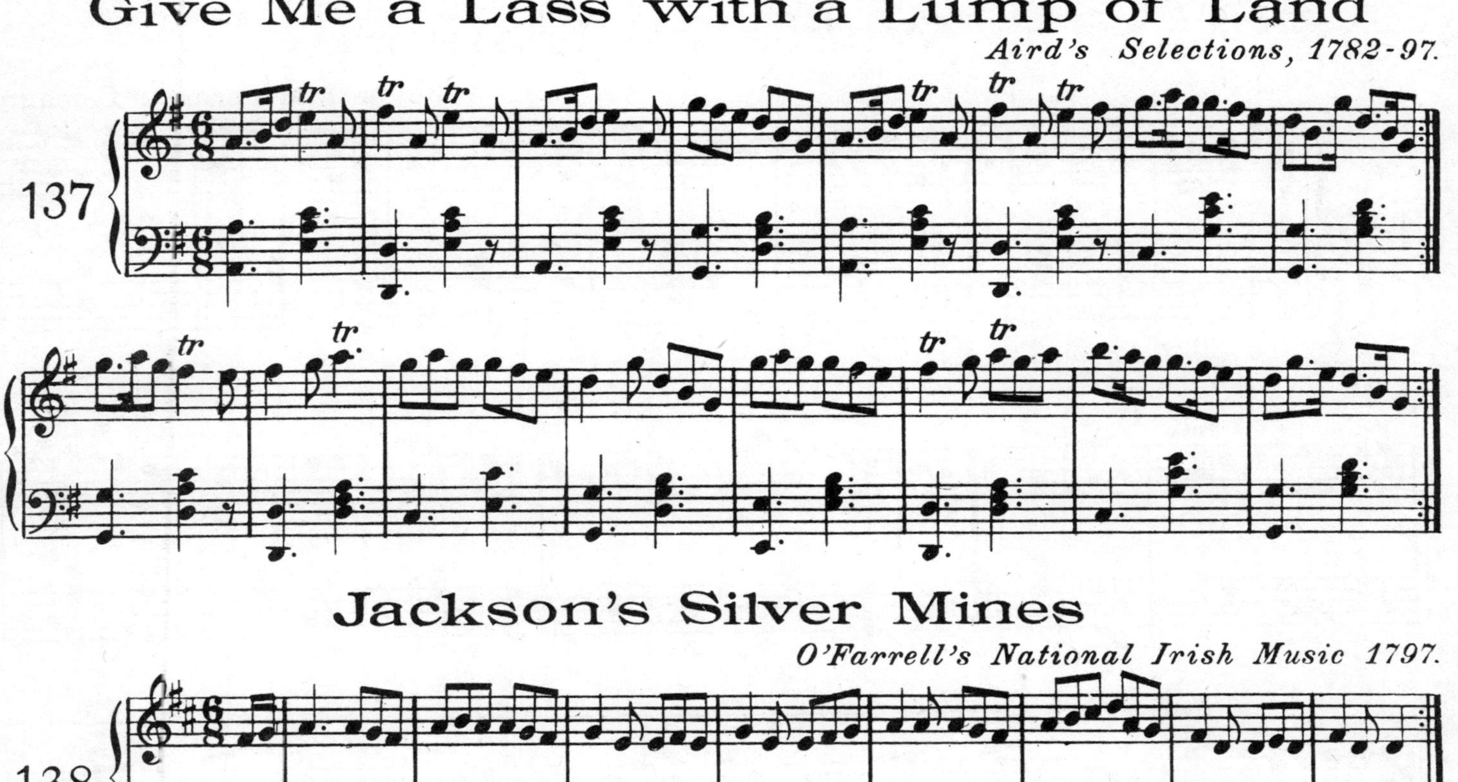

Jackson's Silver Mines

O'Farrell's National Irish Music 1797.

138

Waves of Tramore

Wm. J. McCormick, Chicago.

139

1

2

"The Waves of Tramore," obtained from our versatile friend Mr. McCormick, who swings a bow, or fingers a chanter with equal facility, is a much better jig than "Larry Grogan" of which it is a variant. The latter was composed early in the 18th century by Lawrence Grogan of Johnstown Castle, Kilkenny, a "gentleman piper," celebrated in song and story.

"Larry Grogan" was printed in *Aird's Selection of Scotch, English, Irish and Foreign Airs; Glasgow, 1782;* and in *The Hibernian Muse, London, 1787.* An unmusical second part detracted from its popularity, altho few Irish dance tunes have been favored with such liberal publicity.

A Lilt from Home

Capt. F. O'Neill.

Put in Enough

This is one of the famous "Piper" Jackson's Jigs, not included in any modern collection since its publication in a much higher key in *Cinton's Gems of Ireland; London 1841.*

Dromey's Fancy

This catchy strain which is a superior variant of "The Dancing Master" in *O'Neill's Dance Music of Ireland* was introduced to Chicagoans by John Dromey an excellent fluter, and amateur piper, whose name it bears. Mr. Dromey who is yet hale and hearty, was in his prime, a generation ago, the star of every Irish gathering, for as a traditional singer of Irish songs, he was unrivalled.

Digging for Gold

Sergt. Jas. O'Neill Mss.

143

Petticoat Loose

Sergt. Jas. O'Neill Mss.

144

"Petticoat Loose" is an old name for a dance tune. A jig under that name in *O'Neill's Dance Music of Ireland* bears no resemblance to the above.

Jackson's Frolic

Aird's Selections 1782 - 97

145

An anonymous variant of "Jackson's Frolic" was memorized from the fluting of James Moore in Chicago some fifty years ago. Another version of the tune heard later differed so materially in the second part, that it was added as a third part to Moore's variant, and printed as "Kitty of Oulart" in former O'Neill Collections.

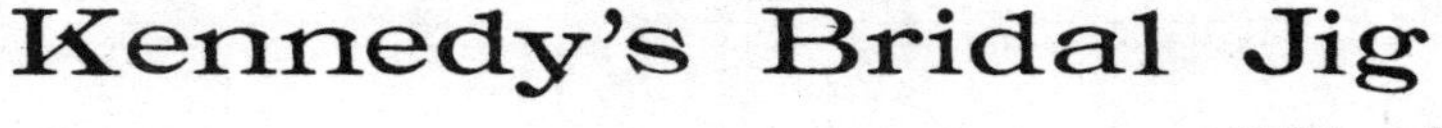

Kennedy's Bridal Jig

Offr. James Kennedy, Chicago.

146

Jackson's Welcome Home

Sergt. Jas. O'Neill Mss.

147

Jackson's Bottle of Claret

Paul Alday's Pocket Volume etc. C. 1800

148

Innis's Jig

Aird's Selections 1782-97

149

Walls of Enniscorthy

An excellent setting of a Double Jig as played by Delaney, Early and McFadden, and of which the above is a popular variant was printed for the first time in the O'Neill Collections 1902-09, and named "The Merry Old Woman."

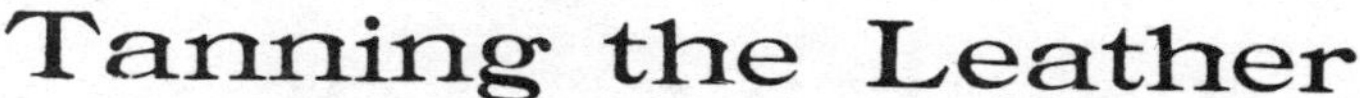

Tanning the Leather

Rice - Walsh, Mss.

151

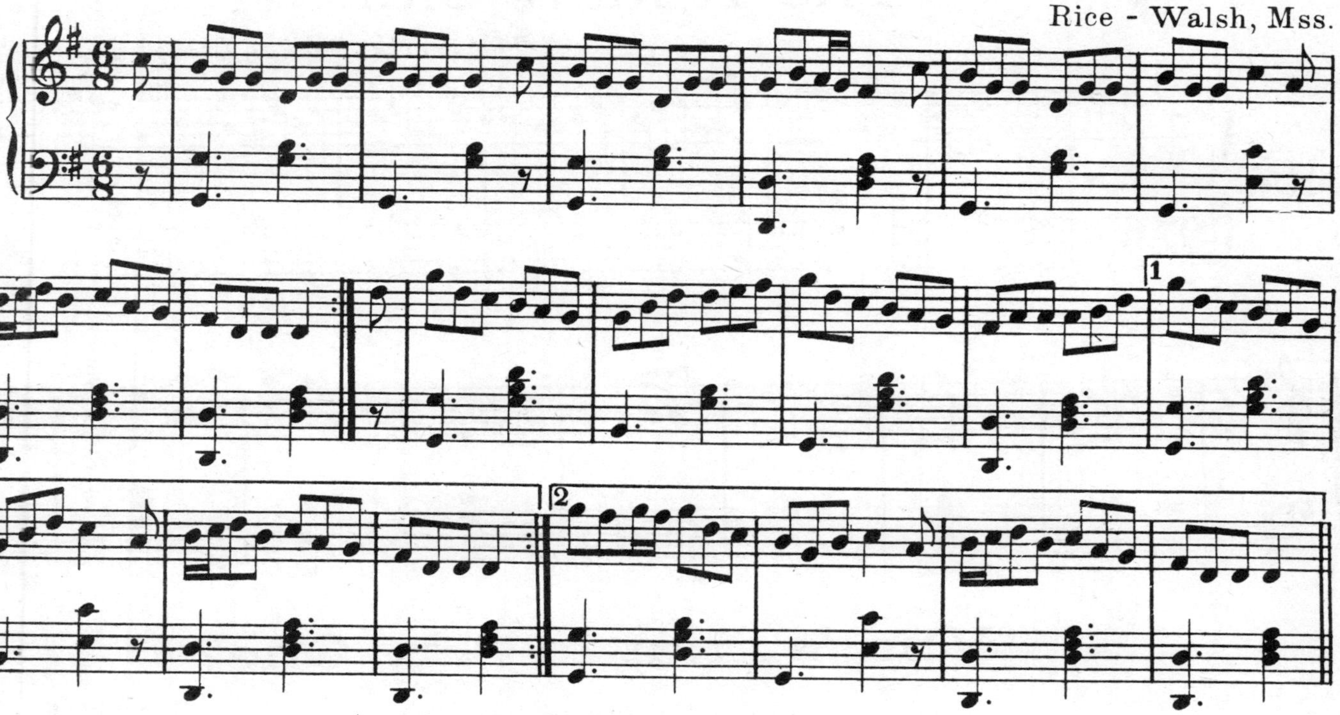

1

2

The Milkmaid

Rice - Walsh, Mss.

152

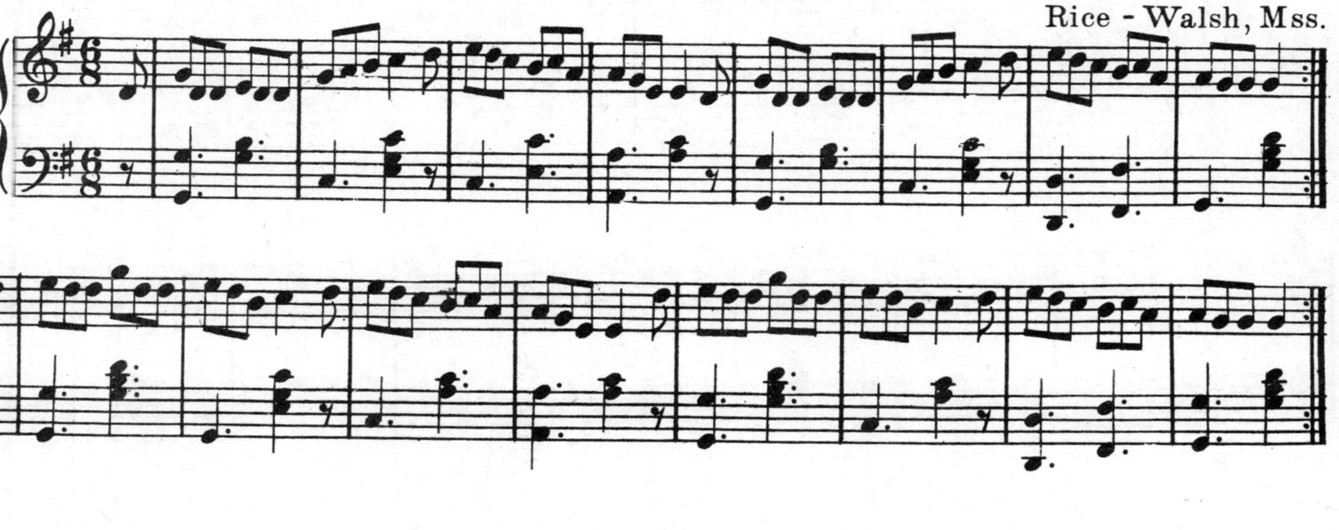

The Far Away Wedding
Capt. F. O'Neill.
153
tr
tr
The Kildare Club
O'Farrell's Pocket Companion 1804-10
154
What's that to Any One?
Capt. F. O'Neill.
155

This fine jig, remarkable for originality of composition, and the technique essential to giving it adequate expression, is a masterpeice of execution at the hands of the amiable Patrick Stack who obligingly scored it on paper, after charming us with it on his fiddle— Coming from Jerry Breen the much admired blind fiddler of North Kerry, it was preserved in the Rice - Walsh Mss. and is new recorded in print for the first time

The Gaelic Club

Capt. F. O'Neill

158

This setting of the "Gaelic Club" differs materially from the "Glasgow Gaelic Club" of the Highlanders, and the "Gaelic Club" Jig in former O'Neill Collections, the second part being new and original.

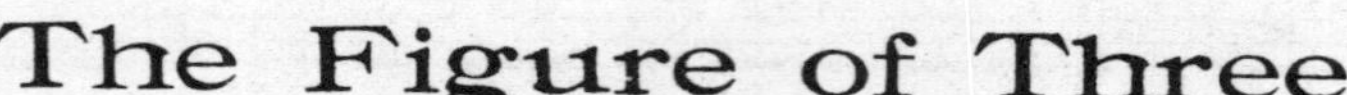

The Figure of Three

Clinton's Gems of Ireland 1841.

159

The Stolen Purse

Capt. F. O'Neill.

160

This rare jig tune which has haunted my memory for years was evidently derived from "The Old Woman Lamenting Her Purse," No. 560, *O'Neill's Music of Ireland, 1903.* The air does not appear in the Bunting Collections. A setting in which the first part is repeated after the second part is printed without note or comment in *Petrie's Complete Collection of Irish Music.*

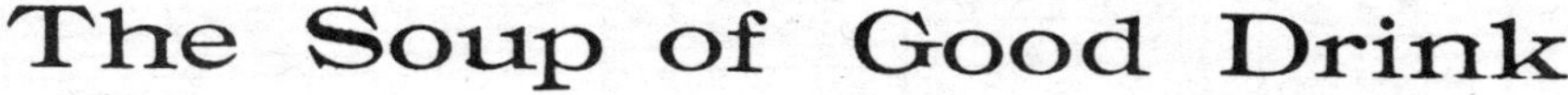

The Soup of Good Drink

O'Farrell's Pocket Companion 1804-10

161

Jackson's Dream

O'Farrell's Pocket Companion 1804-10

162

Jackson's Maid at the Fair

O'Farrells Pocket Companion 1804-10.

The Maids in the Morning

O'Farrell's Pocket Companion 1804-10.

Jackson's Rowly Powly

O'Farrell's Pocket Companion 1804-10.

165

Courtney's Jig

O'Farrell's Pocket Companion 1804-10.

166

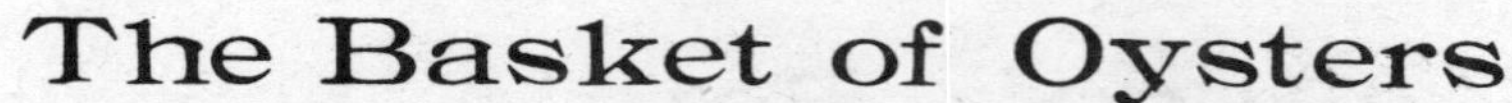

The Basket of Oysters

O'Farrell's Pocket Companion 1804-10.

167

Jackson's Coge in the Morning

O'Farrell's Pocket Companion 1804-10.

168

Fond of the Ladies

Capt. F. O'Neill.

169

Following the example of Dr. Petrie and Dr. Joyce, whose Collections abound in variants, some of which differ but slightly from others in their pages; the editor has continued the practice, rather than risk the loss of a worthy strain. Of that class is "Fond of the Ladies," the opening bars of which remind us of "Sweet Biddy Daly," or, "The Irishman's Heart to the Ladies" previously printed.

The Rover

Capt. F. O'Neill.

170

The Rover is another tune that is suggestive of certain strains with which we are more or less familiar. It proves to be a variant of "Paddy's Resource"— a rather stylish composition printed in former O'Neill Collections.

The Penniless Traveler

Capt. F. O'Neill.

171

The above is an old strain which appeared in print at least as early as 1798 in a much simpler setting under the name "Go to the Devil and Shake Yourself," It was included in six Collections of Country Dances published in London in that year. It has been confused with "Get up Old Woman and Shake Yourself," an entirely different tune. Neither of the names appears in the Bunting, Petrie, or Joyce Collections. Another name for this tune is "When You Are Sick 'Tis Tea You Want," but a tune so named in the Petrie Collections is a different 8 bar melody.

Thomas Galvin - Tralee.

This jig a variant of the much more diversified "Yellow Wattle" No. 853 in *O'Neill's Dance Music of Ireland* was sent me by Prof. P. D. Reilly, a famous dancing master of "London and Castle Island," with the notation—"This simple jig was a noted favorite among the two last generations, and quite good enough for the present when well played."

Fairly Shut of Her

O'Farrell's Pocket Companion 1804-10.

173

Altho McGoun's tune was at hand for years, and was not known to our traditional musicians, I hesitated to claim it as Irish, until O'Farrell specifically notes it as being Irish in his Collection for the Irish or Union Pipes. Few variants while preserving a distinct strain, differ so widely in their development. O'Farrell was a renowned Irish piper who took part in operatic performances on the London stage late in the 18th. century.

Fairly Shot of Her

McGoun's Repository 1803

The Answer I Got

Rice-Walsh, Mss.

Murphy's Weather Eye

Clinton's Irish Melodies 1840

178

The Old Walls of Liscarroll

Prof. P. D. Reidy Mss.

179

In the year 1902 a thin oblong book of Mss. music came to hand from P. D. Reidy "Prof. of Dancing, London and Castleisland." Altho it included forty tunes from the repertory of five competent fiddlers, nearly all were variants of tunes already in our possession. The above as played by Daniel J. Kelleher is one of the exceptions. There can be little doubt that Mr. Reidy's title was well deserved, because his fame as a dancer and dancing master in early life in North Kerry was successfully maintained later in life in London, where he was esteemed as an authority on the subject. Frequent mention of his name appears in *Irish Minstrels and Musicians*.

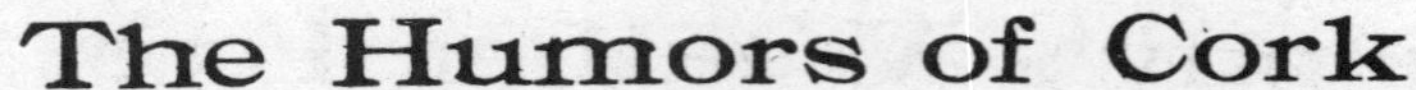

The Humors of Cork

Sergt. Jas. O'Neill Mss.

180

O'Connor's Frolics

Sergt. Jas. O'Neill Mss.

181

The Lasses of Limerick

O'Farrell's Pocket Companion 1804-10.

182

The Female Hero

Aird's Selections 1782-97.

183

Dumfries House

Aird's Selections 1782-97.

184

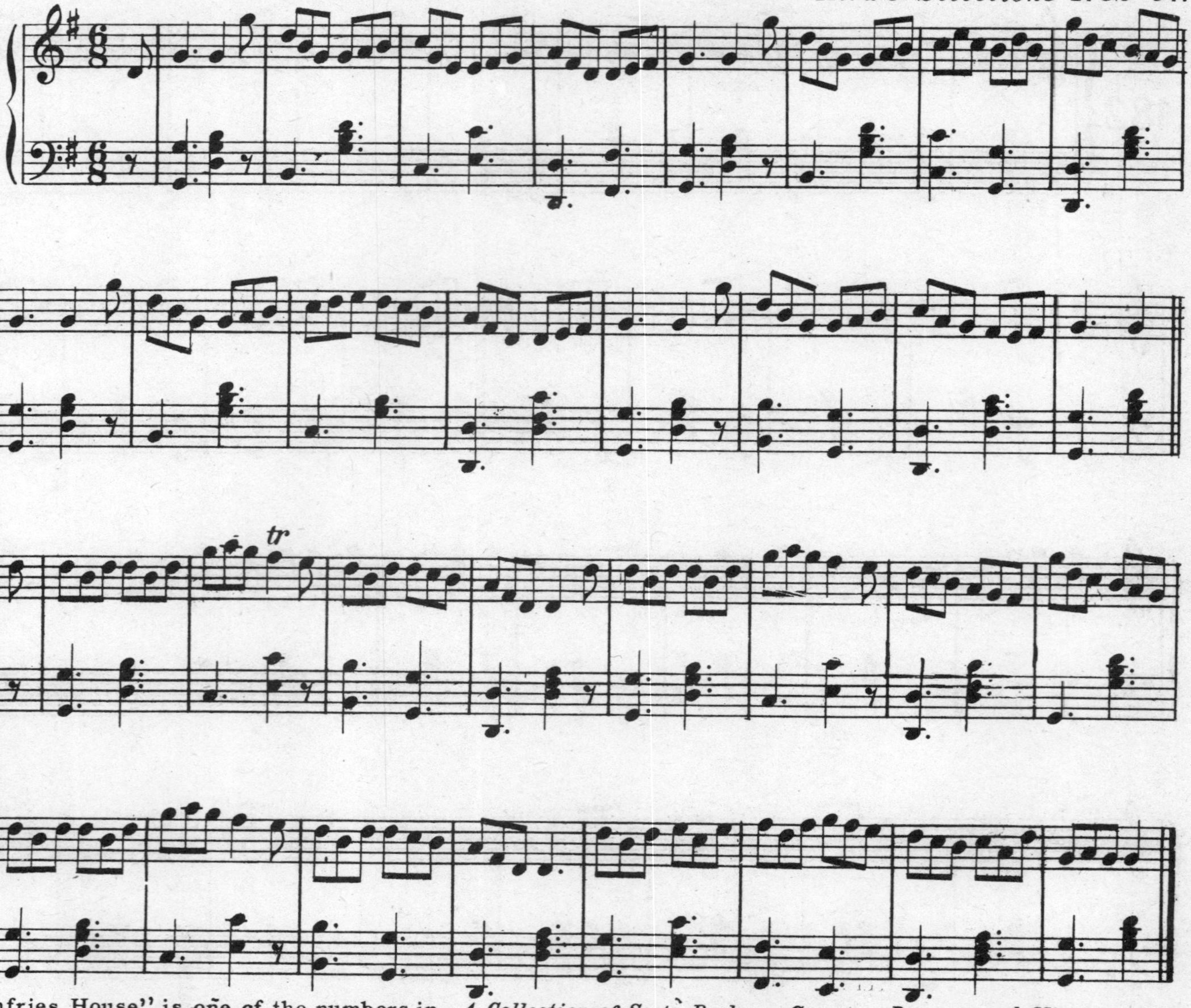

"Dumfries House" is one of the numbers in *A Collection of Scots Reels, or Country Dances, and Minuets etc.* composed by John Riddle at Ayr, and sold by himself about the year 1766.

The Rising Step

Capt. F. O'Neill.

185

The Hare in the Corn

Aird's Selections 1782-97.

186

A rather florid setting of "The Hare in the Corn," procured "from a piper in 1800" is printed in *Bunting's Ancient Music of Ireland,* published in 1840, with notation "Author and date unknown" The name is not indexed in any of the Petrie or Joyce Collections. The setting herewith presented was taken from *Aird's Selection of Scotch, English, Irish, and Foreign Airs, 1782-97.* It is also known as "The Hare in the Corner." It may be permissible to abbreviate such an involved title as "Sae braley as I was kiss'd yestreen" into "Yesterday's Kisses" both for convenience and euphony, especially as the sentiment has not been clouded by the change. This jig preserved also in *Aird's Selections,* has been given circulation recently on the player-pianos.

Yesterday's Kisses

Aird's Selections 1782-97.

187

The Streams of Kilnaspig

Pat. Dunne. Mss.

188

The Skylark

Pat. Dunne. Mss.

189

Jackson's Over the Water

Aird's Selections 1782-97

190

Light and Airy

Neil Gow & Sons Complete Repository, Edinburgh 1805

191

"Light and Airy" first appeared in *A Choice Collection of Scots Reels or Country Dances & Strathspeys etc.*; published by Robert Ross at Edinburgh, 1780.

Hinchy's Fancy

Capt. F. O'Neill

The above Jig named after a blind fiddler of East Clare two generations ago, is a better setting of "Hinchy's Delight," first published in *O'Neill's Music of Ireland of Ireland, 1903*. It was noted down from the whistling of Daniel Rogers in Chicago many years ago.

The Last of the Lot

Capt. F. O'Neill

193

Apples in Winter

Wm. F. Hanafin, Boston

194

A setting of this tune named "Kennedy's Jig" appears in *Joyces Ancient Irish Music Dublin 1890*. Known to the fiddlers and pipers on this side of the Atlantic in later years as "Apples in Winter," it was printed under that name in the O'Neill Collections, but no variant of the popular jig so far in circulation, displays the skill of that played by the versatile "Billy" Hanafin, proficient on both instruments.

It may be pertinent to add that the Jig named "Apples in Winter" in *O'Farrell's Collection of National Irish Music for the Union Pipes, London, 1797*, is identical with "Gillan's Apples" in former O'Neill Collections.

Tumble the Tinker

An excellent double jig called "Tumble the Tinker," was printed for the first time in the enlarged edition of *O'Neills Irish Music for Piano or Violin,* issued in 1915. It was obtained from John McFadden a clever traditional Irish fiddler of Chicago, who until then had forgotten the tune since leaving his native Mayo some forty years before.

Since its publication as stated a spirited second finish has been developed. As varied in the present setting "Tumble the Tinker", heretofore so little known is assuredly worthy of preservation, and enhanced publicity.

Jimmy O'Brien's Jig

The first, third, and fourth parts, of this fine Double Jig were memorized by the editor from the playing of James O'Brien a very capable Irish piper hailing from Mayo, who sojourned in Chicago in 1876. It was printed for the first time on this side of the Atlantic in *O'Neill's Music of Ireland, Chicago, 1903.* A somewhat different setting of it in a much higher key entitled "Copey's Jig – Jackson" was later discovered in *Clinton's Gems of Ireland – 200 Airs – London, 1841.*

Its reproduction in this work is for the purpose of preserving the second part recently introduced in connection with the first as a separate tune. The enlarged arrangement justifies itself.

Capt. F. O'Neill

196

Morrison's Fancy

Capt. F. O'Neill

197

The Splashing of the Churn

Capt. F. O'Neill.

198

This spirited Slip Jig is a variant of "Dublin Streets," obtained from Mr. Ennis of the Irish Music Club of Chicago, and published in former O'Neill Collections. "The Splashing of the Churn," or in Irish "*Glugur an Meadair*" is the original name of the tune.

Following is another version of it, obtained thru the courtesy of Sergt. James P. Walsh of Chicago whose Mss. collection has been a prolific source of many desirable melodies hitherto unpublished.

Humors of Bottle Hill

Sergt. James P. Walsh.

199

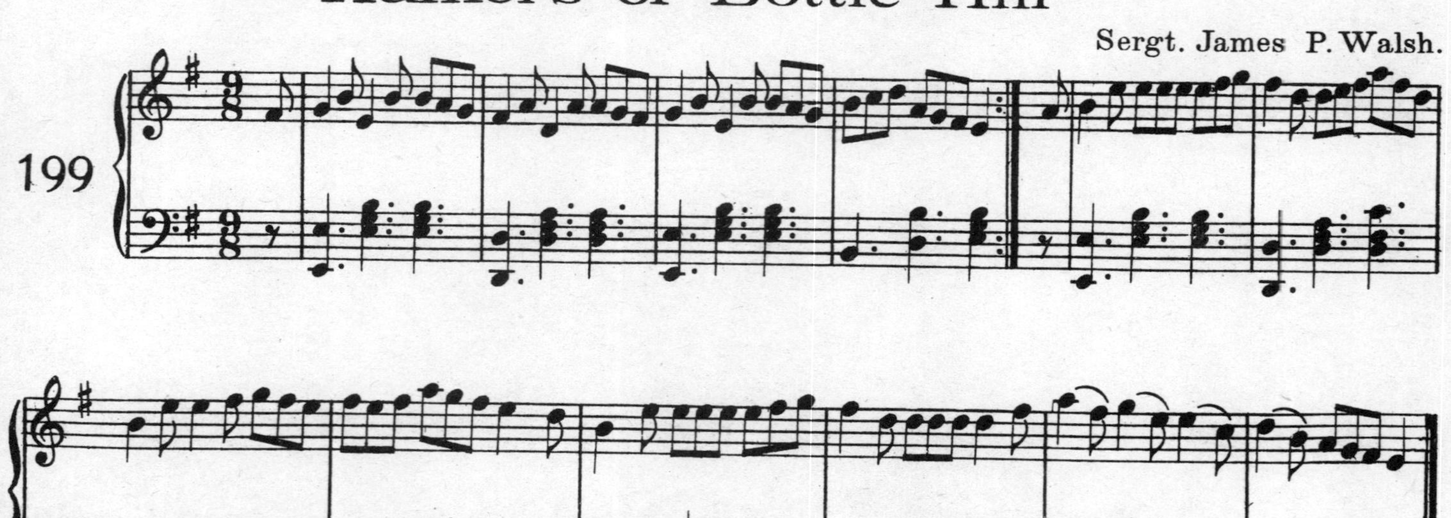

The Good Fellow
Sergt. Jas. O'Neill. Mss.
200
Miss Brown's Fancy
Sergt. Jas. O'Neill. Mss.
201
The Irish Hop Pickers
Wilon's Companion to the Ballroom, 1816.
202

The Kitten

O'Farrell's Pocket Companion 1804-10.

203

Dolly's the Girl for Me

Aird's Selections 1782-97.

204

Mc Donnell's Rant
O'Farrell's National Irish Music 1797.
205
1
2
1
2
D.S.
Yellow Stockings
O'Farrell's National Irish Music 1797.
206
Darby Carey
O'Farrell's Pocket Companion 1804-10.
207

Gilla Machree

"The Piper's Maggot," as this old tune was called, first appeared in print in *Robt. Bremner's Collection of Scots Reels and Country Dances, Edinburgh 1758.* As the word "Maggot" which means an odd fancy or whim is obsolete in this age, the change of name is permissible.

The tune was printed in *Aird's Selections etc. London 1797,* and in later publications somewhat varied.

The Lasses of Sligo
Powers' Musical Cabinet 1810.
210
Capt. McDonald's Favorite
O'Farrell's Pocket Companion 1804-10.
211
Come to the Bridal
Aird's Selections 1782-97.
212

The Munster Rake

O'Farrell's Pocket Companion 1804-10.

213

The Long Room

Aird's Selections 1782-97.

214

Lasses of Solohod

Rice-Walsh Mss.

215

The above is a variant of "The Rakes of Solohod" No. 454 *O'Neill's Dance Music of Ireland.*

The Roving Blade

Rice-Walsh Mss.

216

A Fig for a Kiss

Preston's Selection of Reels & Country Dances London 1768.

217

Reels

Lady Kelly's Reel
(or Up Roscommon!)

As played by John Kelly of San Francisco

218

D.C.

This famous reel as played by John Kelly a fiddler of phenomenal execution now living in San Francisco Cal. is a florid setting of Sergt. James O'Neill's "Northern Lasses" printed in the O'Neill Collections Kelly a native of Roscommon, Ireland, says this reel was known as "Kelly's Reel" before his time. It was his masterly rendering of "Lady Kelly's Reel" that won the championship for Owen Brennan an expert piper, as described on page 215. *Irish Minstrels and Musicians.*

Miss Corbett's Reel
Aird's Selections 1782-97
219
The Sweetheart Reel
Capt. F. O'Neill
220
Kitty O'Neill
Capt. F. O'Neill
221
D.S.

Mamma's Pet

Capt. F. O'Neill.

222

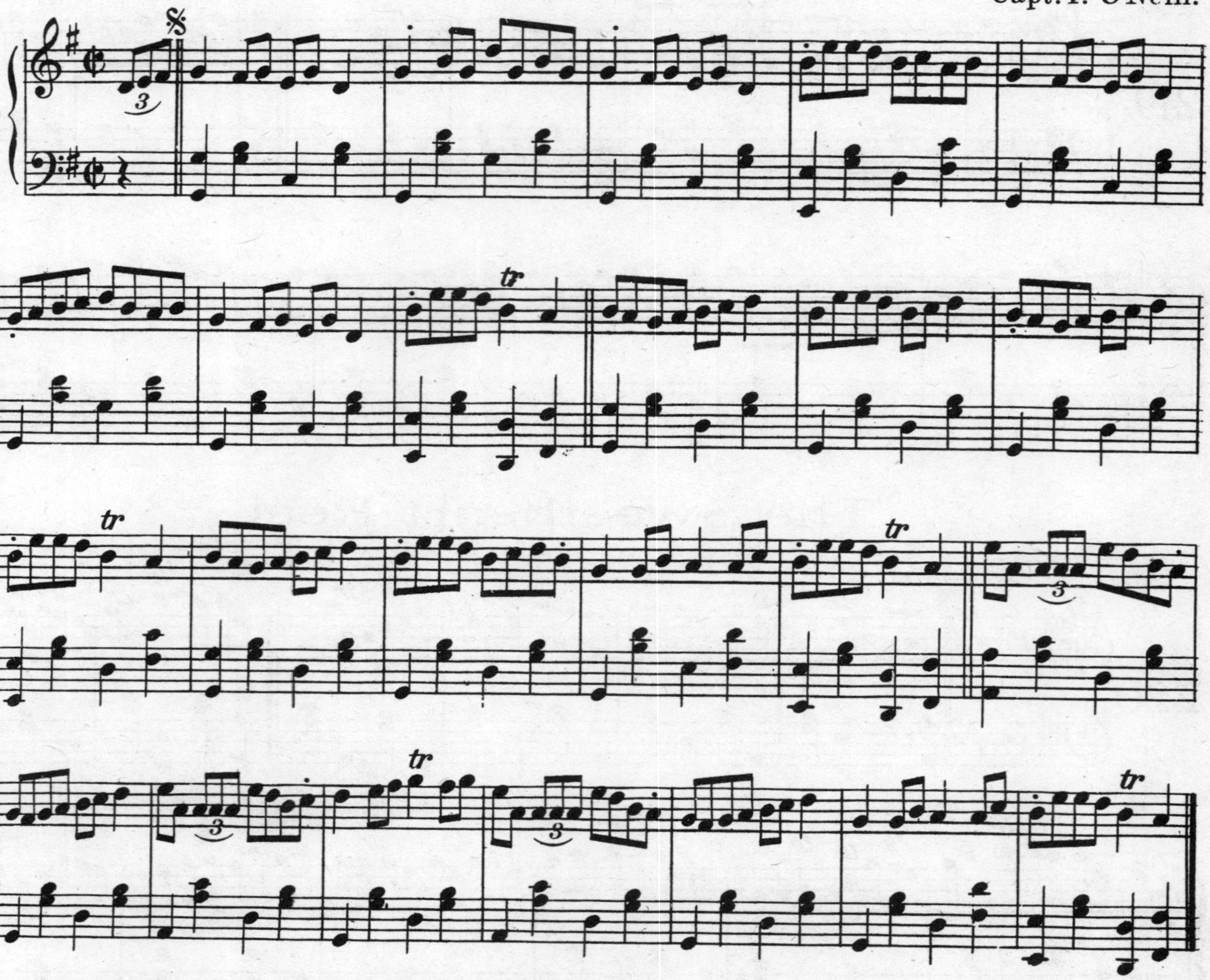

In boyhood days I memorized the first part of this reel from the fiddle playing of Mr. Downing a gentleman farmer who taught me the rudiments of music on the flute. Thirty-five years later the second part was supplied by A.S. Beamish, another West Cork musician. Being without a name the tune was called "Timothy Downing," or "Downing's Reel," in the O'Neill Collections. With a third part obtained from the famous fiddler John McFadden of Mayo, this tripartite reel is presented under its presumably true name.

The Glenmore Hunt

O'Farrell's Pocket Companion, 1804-10.

223

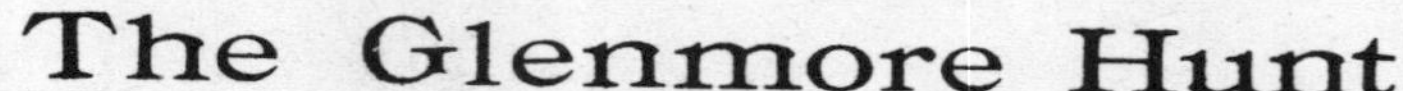

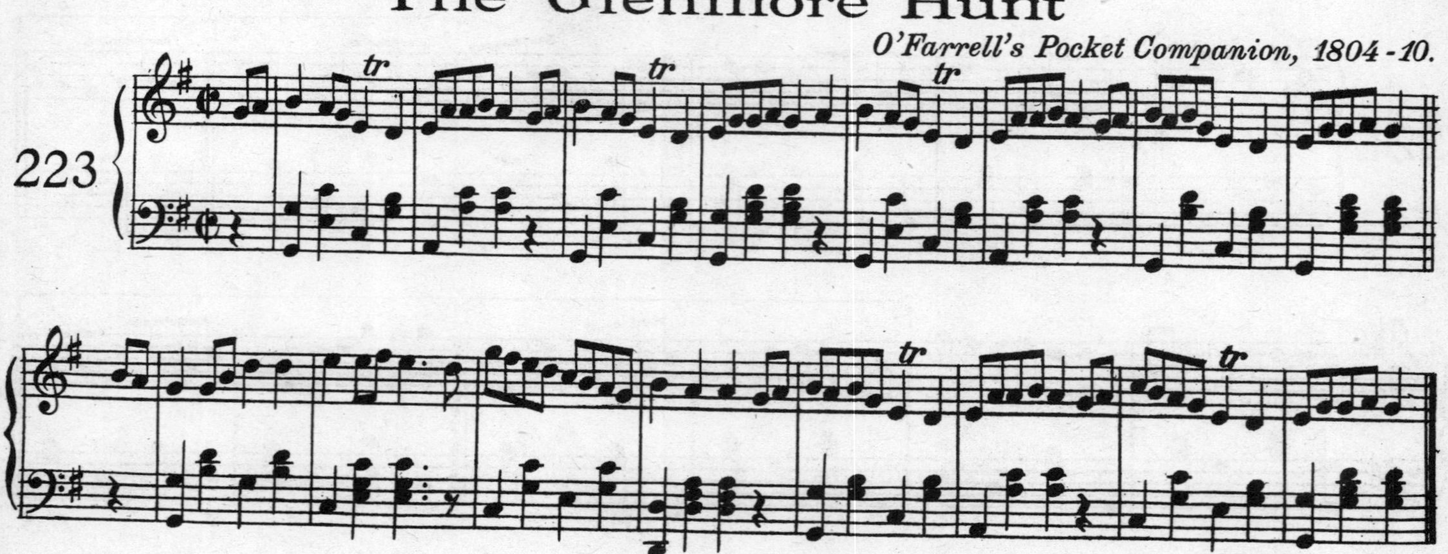

The Four-Hand Reel

Capt. F. O'Neill

224

"The Four Hand Reel" as far as the writer is aware was first brought to Chicago in 1886 by "Barney" Delaney, an excellent Irish piper. So versatile was he, like most great Irish musicians, in the manipulation of his instrument, that he varied his tunes according to fancy without detriment to tone or rhythm, but rather to the advantage of the general effect. Although not included in any collection of Irish music published beyond the Atlantic, the strain must have been quite popular in the Eastern States, for we find the tune in a Boston publication no less than four times, and named respectively; "Corporal Casey's Favorite," "Lady Gardner's Reel," "Parnell's Reel," and "Yellow-haired Laddie." All consisting of but two parts each.

The setting here presented was memorized from Delaney's playing, but no bare scoring of measured bars could do justice to his inimitable execution.

Since the foregoing was written I find that "The Five-Mile Chase" in *R.M. Levey's Second Collection of the Dance Music of Ireland, London, 1873;* consisting of but two parts, is also a variant of "The Four-Hand Reel."

The Marquis of Huntly's Reel

Mc. Goun's Repository C. 1803

225

This fine reel first published in 1781 is but one of many composed by Wm. Marshall who for thirty years was in the service of the Duke of Gordon as butler and house steward. In music as in other accomplishments he was entirely self taught. His playing of strathspeys, and reels was so inspiring, it is said, that neither the old nor the young could overcome their inclination to dance. As an amateur violin player of Scottish dance music, he was unrivalled in the last half of the 18th. century. No composer of his time was so victimized by plagiarists who appropriated his tunes, changed a few notes, and passed them off as their own under different titles.

Capt. Keller's Reel

Mc. Goun's Repository C. 1803

226

The above clever tune first appeared in 1761 in *A Collection of the Newest and the Best Reels and Country Dances* published in Edinburgh by Neil Stewart. As "Capt. Keeler's Reel" it has been reprinted in recent years, but without the spirited second finish.

Miss Bain's Reel

Aird's Selections, 1782-97

A Letter from Home

Capt. F. O'Neill

230

Miss Gunning's Delight

Aird's Selections, 1782-97

231

Well-born and of surpassing loveliness only equalled by their poverty, the famous Gunning sisters, Maria and Elizabeth born in Roscommon, and educated in Dublin, became Lady Coventry, and Duchess of Hamilton respectively, in 1752, one year after their arrival in London. The marriages of "two Irish girls of no fortune who are declared the handsomest women alive," were great public events. "May the luck of the Gunnings attend you," was a proverbial Irish blessing.

The above setting of a tune composed in their honor, and printed in *Aird's Selection of Scotch, English, Irish, and Foreign Airs;* vol. 1-1782 is doubtless the original. A highly elaborate and difficult variant in four parts found in Sergt. James O'Neill's Mss. entitled "The Contradiction" was printed in former O'Neill Collections. As an example of what may be developed from a simple composition by a skilful hand, both original and variant are herewith submitted for comparison.

The Contradiction
(Miss Gunning's Delight Variant)

Sergt. Jas. O'Neill

232

A few years ago as Mr. Leech was fingering a stray reel on his flute, Prof John Cummings (mentioned on page 282-4 *Irish Minstrels and Musicians*) remarked "that's 'The Raveled Hank of Yarn' and I had forgotten it for the last forty years." Although then in his 85th year he buckled on his pipes, and played the tune in a style which astonished his audience. It is a variant of No. 638, *O'Neills Dance Music of Ireland*.

Green Grows the Rashes

Neil Gow & Son's Complete Repository C.1805

Robert Burns' song to this oldtime favorite strain, was in general circulation among the Irish peasantry early in the last century, and the name is still well remembered. The melody much older than the poet's day, was known as "We're a' dry wi' drinking o't!" In reel time it was first printed in 1761, by Neil Stewart of Edinburgh in *A Collection of the Newest, and Best Reels, or Country Dances, Adapted for the Violin or German Flute.* The traditional Irish version of the tune as remembered by the editor may prove not uninterestin- to the musical student of a later generation.

Green Grows the Rushes O

Capt. F. O'Neill

235

Jack Lattin with Variations

O'Farrell's National Irish Music 1797

236

(Jack Lattin) Continued

The renowned Walter Jackson popularly known as "Piper" Jackson who flourished about the middle of the 18th century, was reputed to be the composer of "Jack Lattin", "Jack O'Lattan", or "Jacky Latin", as the tune has been variously called. Under the first name it was printed in *Waylet's Collection of Country Dances, 1749*. As "Jack Laten" I find an elaborate setting of it in *Mc Gibbon's Collection of Scots Tunes* published in London 1755 consisting of four original parts apparently, and fifteen variations. While preserving the same strain, but more suitable to our purpose, O'Farrell's setting of much later date is here presented.

A tune known to me as "Jenny Rock the Cradle" was declared to be "Jacky Latin" by a musical acquaintance, and it was under the latter name it was printed in *O'Neill's Dance Music of Ireland* in 1907.

If both tunes were derived from Jackson's original composition, they furnish a striking illustration of how time, taste, and development diversify a strain of music in a few generations.

Jennie Rock the Cradle

Capt. F. O'Neill

237

The Moniemusk Reel (WITH VARIATIONS)

Capt. F. O'Neill.

238

D.S.

The origin or meaning of the name of this popular tune defied investigation and inquiry for many years. Eventually a glance thru the pages of *McGoun's Repository of Scots and Irish airs, Strathspeys, Reels, etc; Glasgow, 1803* led to the solution of the puzzle. Among the contents was "Sir Archibald Grant of Moniemusk's Reel." The popular name Moniemusk was that of an estate, and the full name of the reel being inconveniently long, it was abbreviated to "Moniemusk" and the rest of the name forgotten. The first and second parts as above noted constitute the original tune as composed by Daniel or Donald Dow, a musician of note who died at Edinburgh in 1783. The third was substituted for the more difficult second by modern fiddlers, and the fourth, the editor memorized from the playing of Wm. McLean the greatest Highland piper of his day in Chicago, some fifty years ago.

Charming Mary Kelly

Capt. F. O'Neill.

The Early Rose

Rice–Walsh Mss.

240

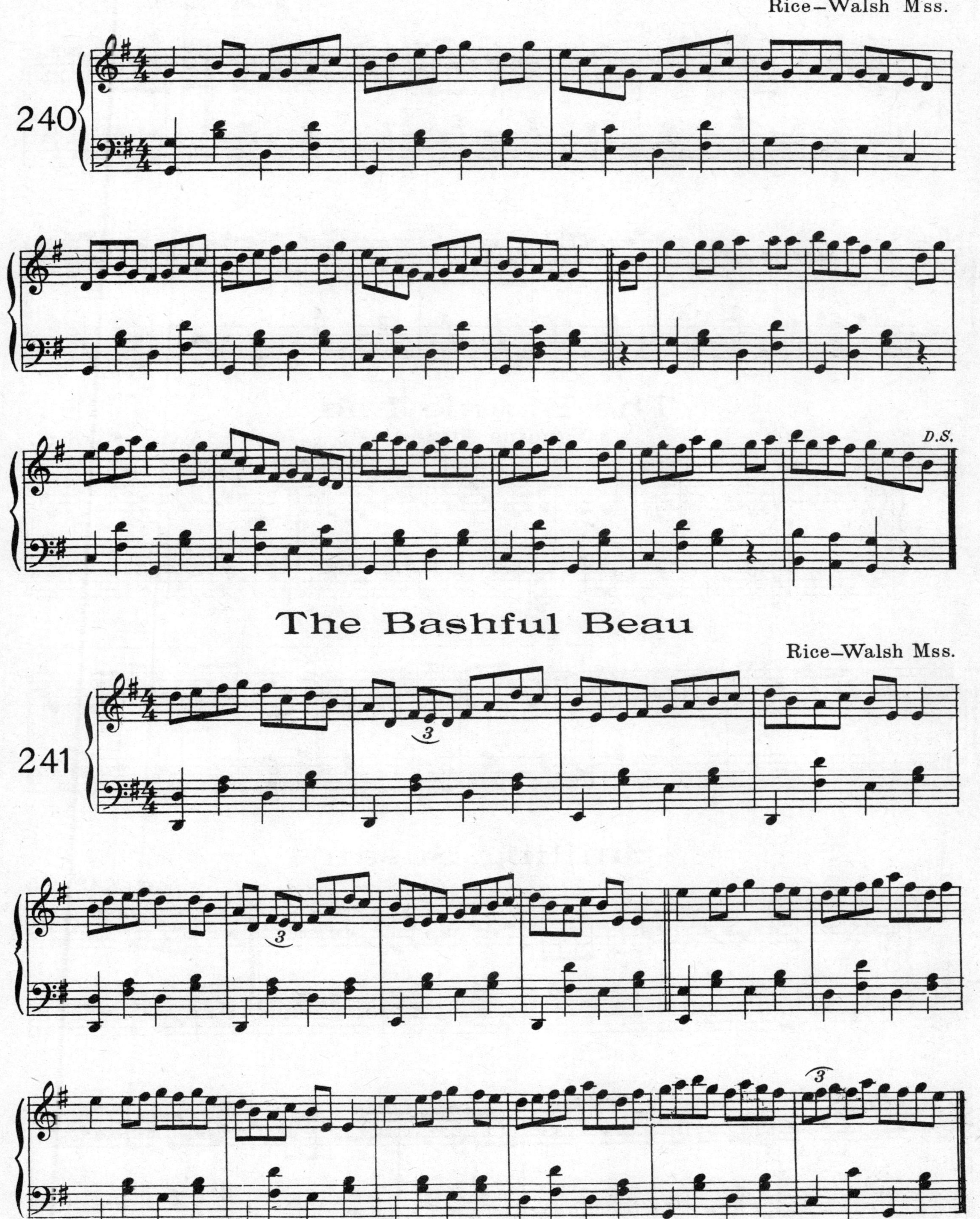

The Bashful Beau

Rice–Walsh Mss.

241

Because I Was a Bonnie Lad
Aird's Selections 1782-97.
242
The Bonnie Lad
(Warpipe Style.)
Capt. F. O'Neill.
243
Smiling Susan
Capt. F. O'Neill.
244

The Fairy Hurlers
or Walsh's Favorite

By Joseph P. Tamony and John Kelly } San Francisco Cal.

According to legendary lore the fairies or good people enjoy the same activities and pastimes especially hurling, and dancing, as they did before being called to another life. Many a tale is told of their kidnapping a competent piper when necessary to entertain them at their festivities in the subterranean quarters they are said to occupy within the ancient raths or forts so numerous all over Ireland.

The Fairy Faith still survives

The Maids of Tipperary
Pat. Dunne Mss.
246
How We Spent the Christmas
Capt. F. O'Neill
247
I Wish You Would Marry Me Now
Preston's Collection of Scots Reels and Country Dances 1768
248

The Factory Lass

Miss Theresa Geary, Chicago

"The Factory Lass" was first heard by the editor at Gaelic Park Chicago on July 4th '22. It was cleverly rendered in concert by Mr. Mullaney, Miss Geary, and Mr. McGrath, on the Irish or Union Pipes, Violin, and Flute, respectively. The similarity of strain, especially in the first part to that of the "Home-Made Reel" which follows may be noticed.

Home-Made Reel

Capt. F. O'Neill

250

"The Rose Garden" is entirely distinct from "The Rose in the Garden" in former O'Neill Collections.

Turkey in the Straw

John McFadden.

254

"Turkey in the Straw," or "Old Zip Coon," as played nowadays may suit the rapid movements of buck-dancers, but the frenzied rhythm is ruinous to the melody. Rendered after the manner of the famous Dan Emmett of Bryant's Minstrels, in slow reel time, this popular tune acquires a much enhanced appeal. Emmett, it will be remembered was the author of the immortal "Dixie," and it was his version of "Turkey in the Straw," which we obtained from John McFadden of the Chicago Irish Music Club, that is here presented. The origin of this favorite of our fathers is wrapped in even deeper mystery than that of "Yankee Doodle". Under the title "Old Zip Coon" the tune appeared in Howe's Collections about the middle of the 19th century, and possibly earlier. The first gleam of light on the question of how the old title eventually yielded to the popularity of the new name, came through a chance conversation while fishing in 1920 with a northern tourist at Ocean Springs, Mississippi. The latter confidently informed me that Alderman Silas Leachman of Chicago, a native of Kentucky was the author of "Turkey in the Straw"—both words and music! The melody I knew was older than the Alderman's grandfather, yet here was a lead worth investigating, for it was his melodious voice that first brought him into prominence. An interview with the talented official at Chicago a month later confirmed the statement that he was indeed the author of *one* song of that name—the best of several others on the same theme. One question was settled. The popularity of the modern song relegated to obscurity the name of the ancient tune. The pioneers or early settlers of West Virginia, Kentucky, and Tennessee, were largely of Irish ancestry, and obviously their music or tunes more or less varied by fancy, and defective memorizing from one generation to another, were of Irish origin. Fiddling and dancing being inseparable from all festivities and important events, the tunes became much more diversified, but the swing and spirit of the Gael however was always discernable in their reels and quadrilles, and so continues to the present day.

For the convenience of musical antiquaries who may be interested in the subject, an old Irish March, or Jig, "The Kinnegad Slashers" to which is sung "The Land of Sweet Erin," is herewith submitted as a tune from which "Old Zip Coon" or "Turkey in the Straw" could have been derived or evolved. A third part added by later musicians is not essential in this illustration.

The Kinnegad Slashers

O'Farrell's Pocket Companion for the Irish or Union Pipes. 1804-10.

The Arkansas Traveler

Capt. F. O'Neill.

Vying in popularity with "Turkey in the Straw," another American favorite claims our attention. Famous in song and story its origin has baffled investigation. An exhaustive research conducted by Dr. H. C. Mercer, an official of Buck's County Historical Society (Doylestown, Pa.) relating to its history and antecedents failed of its purpose. All lines of inquiry extending to Kentucky, Arkansas, and Louisiana, ended in contradiction, and uncertainty. Futhermore; the quaint dialogue between the "Traveler" and the backwoods fiddler was based on nothing more substantial than a fertile imagination. The opening paragraph of Dr. Mercer's essay published in the Century Magazine— *On the Track of the Arkansas Traveler* — is well worth quoting: "Sometime about the year 1850 the American musical myth known as "The Arkansas Traveler" came into vogue among fiddlers. It is a quick reel tune with a backwoods story talked to it while played, that caught the ear at sideshows and circuses, and sounded over the trodden turf of fair grounds. Bands and foreign-bred musicians were above noticing it, but the people loved it, and kept time to it, while tramps and sailors carried it across seas to vie merrily in Irish cabins with "The Wind that Shakes the Barley," and "The Soldier's Joy."

Though classed as a reel, the tune as printed with Dr. Mercer's clever essay and elsewhere, is scored as a buckdance, and in a key much too low for certain instruments. The editor who is responsible for the setting above presented ventures to suggest that like "Old Zip Coon" or "Turkey in the Straw" "The Arkansas Traveler" had been evolved from a venerable Irish strain by some backwoods fiddler whose identity is lost in the oblivion which engulfed the composers of the multitude of Irish melodies that have survived many influences inimical to their preservation.

Among the probable sources from which the tune in question may have been derived are the following examples:

The Priest and His Boots

O'Neill's Dance Music of Ireland. 1907.

As "The Priest in his Boots" and "The Parson in his Boots," this tune was printed in six different Collections of Music between the years 1765, and 1809, at Edinburgh, London, and Dublin. The dullest ear can discern the similarity of strain in the second parts of "The Priest and his Boots" and "The Arkansas Traveler."

Compare the first part of "The Arkansas Traveler" with the first part of No. 559, *O'Neill's Dance Music of Ireland,* which follows.

Johnny with the Queer Thing

A study of another fine old reel No. 752 of the same volume, named "The Queen's Shilling" but known in Scotland as "Lady Mary Ramsay" fosters the idea that perhaps there was nothing so very remarkable after all in the Traveler's completing the tune for the pioneer Paganini.

The Queen's Shilling

O'Neill's Dance Music of Ireland. 1907.

Cameron House

Aird's Selections 1782-97

I saw this tune in M.S. written in West Cork early in the 19th century. The fact remains that it had been preserved in printer's ink in *Bremner's Collection of Scots Reels, or Country Dances, Edinburgh 1757*. Its oldtime popularity is attested by its inclusion in several other worthy Collections long out of print, such as, *The Caledonian Muse 1785*; and *Neil Gow and Sons' Complete Repository etc; 1805.*

Delaney's Frolics

Capt. F. O'Neill

259

The Rolling Reel

Capt. F. O'Neill

260

The Golden Wedding

Capt. F. O'Neill

261

Miss Farr's Reel
Pat. Dunne, Mss.
262
Irish Pat
Pat. Dunne, Mss.
263
The Donegal Reel
Pat. Dunne, Mss.
264

Dunse Dings All

Aird's Selections 1782-97

From Glen's Analytical Table we learn that a tune named "Dunse Dings A'," was printed in *Neil Stewart's A Collection of the Newest and the Best Reels, or Country Dances Adapted for the Violin or German Flute. Edinburgh 1761-62.* Dunse a town in the Lowlands, a few miles from the English Border gave name to several tunes. "Dunse Dings A'" signifies in plain English; Dunse surpasses or excels all, an exaggerated yet pardonable expression of local pride.

Never Grow Old

Capt. F. O'Neill

Tickle the Strings

Patrick Stack, Chicago

267

Limber Elbow

Patrick Stack, Chicago

268

Cabar Feigh, or The Deers' Horns

Setting by John Kelly, San Francisco

269

When first received with a batch of fine tunes noted down by our unselfish friend Francis E. Walsh from the playing of clever San Francisco musicians, the foregoing reel under a slightly different name was recognized as a variant of "Rakish Paddy" previously printed in *The Music of Ireland;* and *O'Neill's Dance Music of Ireland*. Another variant named "Sporting Pat" is to be found in *O'Neill's Irish Music, for Piano or Violin*. Under the circumstances, another variant seemed superfluous, but coming from such a famous fiddler as John Kelly of Roscommon, it has been cheerfully welcomed to our pages.

A favorite with all capable pipers and fiddlers of our acquaintance for many years, the tune under any of its recognized names does not appear in the Bunting, Petrie, or Joyce publications. As "Caper Fey" it was printed in *Bremner's Second Collection of Scots Reels or Country Dances; London 1768;* yet omitted from *The Glen Collection of Scottish Dance Music, Edinburgh 1891.*

Most Highland Bagpipe note books include a suitable setting of the tune under the correct title as above, in Gaelic and English.

Kelly's Number Two
John Kelly, San Francisco
270
Jerry O'Reilly's Reel
Jerry O'Reilly, San Francisco
271
Seymour's Fancy
Wilson's Companion to the Ballroom 1816
272

I'll Go No More to Yon Town

Sergt. Jas. O'Neill Mss.

273

Popular since its first publication in *Bremner's Collection of Scots Reels, or Country Dances 1757*, "I'll gae nae mair to yon town" has been a fruitful source of variants which circulated under various titles. The variant herewith presented, was found without a name in Sergt. O'Neill's Mss.

Miss Singleton's Reel

Sergt. Jas. O'Neill Mss.

274

The Lady's Earring
Sergt. Jas. O'Neill Mss.
275
D. C.
The Game of Love
Sergt. Jas. O'Neill Mss.
276
D.S.

Dolly Dimple

Rice-Walsh Mss.

277

Morning Cheer

Rice-Walsh Mss.

278

This is a variant of "Jim Moore's Fancy" in *O'Neill's Dance Music of Ireland, 1907*

Colonel Mc Bain's Reel

Rice-Walsh Mss.

279

"Col. Mc Bain's Reel" first appeared in print in *Bremner's 2nd Collection of Scots Reels, or Country Dances, London 1768,* and reprinted in *Mc Goun's Repository of Scots and Irish; Strathspeys, Reels etc; Glasgow 1803.* Its popularity was not confined to Scotland for we find it named "Duke of Clarence Reel" in *Lavenu's New Country Dances for the year 1798,* published at London. A setting of this noted reel as played by the experts of the Irish Music Club of Chicago may be found on page 116 of *O'Neill's Dance Music of Ireland*.

In composition and fluency of rhythm the variant above presented compares very favorably with the original especially when given expression on the fiddle in the inimitable style of the genial "Paddy" Stack from whom the manuscript was obtained.

Free and Easy

Rice-Walsh Mss.

280

The Clever Colleen

Rice-Walsh Mss.

281

The Caledonian Hunt

Aird's Selections, 1782-97

282

This favorite first appeared in *Ross' Choice Collection of Scots Reels Country Dances and Strathspeys. Edinburgh, 1780.*

Colonel Mc Bain's Reel

Rice-Walsh Mss.

279

"Col. Mc Bain's Reel" first appeared in print in *Bremner's 2nd Collection of Scots Reels, or Country Dances, London 1768,* and reprinted in *Mc Goun's Repository of Scots and Irish; Strathspeys, Reels etc; Glasgow 1803.* Its popularity was not confined to Scotland for we find it named "Duke of Clarence Reel" in *Lavenu's New Country Dances for the year 1798,* published at London. A setting of this noted reel as played by the experts of the Irish Music Club of Chicago may be found on page 116 of *O'Neill's Dance Music of Ireland.*

In composition and fluency of rhythm the variant above presented compares very favorably with the original especially when given expression on the fiddle in the inimitable style of the genial "Paddy" Stack from whom the manuscript was obtained.

Free and Easy

Rice-Walsh Mss.

280

is favorite first appeared in *Ross' Choice Collection of Scots Reels Country Dances and Strathspeys.* *inburgh, 1780.*

The Wink of Her Eye

Rice-Walsh Mss.

283

Johnny When You Die

Rice-Walsh Mss.

284

The above is a variant of "Well May the Keel Row," a North of England song tune. It is not listed in Glen's Analytical Table of old Scotch dance tunes. As "Jenny's Frolics" it appears in Vol.2 *Paul Alday's A Pocket Volume of Airs, Duets, Songs, Marches etc. Dublin C 1800.*

The Curragh Races

Capt. F. O'Neill

285

In former O'Neill publications John Mc Fadden's setting of this reel was given preference, being in the florid style of that famous traditional fiddler. The version here presented memorized from lilting by the editor in schoolboy days, may not be devoid of interest especially as the arrangement is suited to the scale of the Highland or Irish warpipes.

The Templehouse Reel

Capt. F. O'Neill

286

Altho the "Templehouse Reel" first appeared in print in the O'Neill Collections, a more fluent setting of it memorized from the playing of "Jimmy" O'Brien may be permissible. The latter, dealt with at considerable length in *Irish Minstrels and Musicians* hailed from the County Mayo, and was a very tasty performer on the Irish or Union pipes. He died at Chicago in 1885.

Miss Wardlaw's Reel

Aird's Selections 1782-97

Greig's Pipes

O'Farrell's Pocket Companion 1804-10

I first heard of this tune twenty odd years ago, as being a favorite with James Quinn an oldtime Chicago piper, familiarly known as "Old Man Quinn." Altho Sergt. Early his relative and pupil had learned it, the tune never got into circulation among musicians. Being unfavorably impressed by the version of "Greig's Pipes" received with other tunes subsequently from Pat. Dunne of Kilbraugh, Tipperary, it was not included among the 1001 Gems in *O'Neill's Dance Music of Ireland.*

The piper in whose honor the tune had been named must have been a noteworthy performer, for almost identical with the setting in *O'Farrell's Pocket Companion for the Irish or Union Pipes*, is another in *A Complete Repository of Old and New Scotch Strathspeys, Reels and Jigs, Selected from the Works of Neil Gow and Sons. Edinburgh 1805.*

As the talented Neil Gow was much inclined to plagiarism, and from the fact that the tune in question had been previously printed by Neil Stewart in 1762 and as early as 1779 by Joshua Campbell "in a Collection of Reels composed by himself" we may assume that Campbell's claim to the composition of "Greig's Pipes" is indisputable.

This tune is a variant of "Tie the Bonnet" in *O'Neill's Dance Music of Ireland, 1907*

Darling Dan

Rice-Walsh Mss.

292

Crossing the Field

Rice-Walsh Mss.

293

Curly Mike

Rice-Walsh Mss.

294

Humors of Ballyheige

Rice-Walsh Mss.

295

Fickle Fortune
Rice-Walsh Mss.
296
The Devil to Pay
Rice-Walsh Mss.
297

The Wallace Twins
Rice-Walsh Mss.
298
Mickey Rattley's Fancy
Rice-Walsh Mss.
299
Limerick Lads
Rice-Walsh Mss.
300

New Year's Night

Capt. F. O'Neill

301

This reel memorized probably from "Barney" Delaney's wonderful piping seems to have been omitted from former O'Neill Collections.

Cuttie Sark

Sergt. Jas. O'Neill, Mss.

302

Though plainly of Scotch origin both in name and tone, "Cuttie Sark" is not to be found in any of the old Scotch or Miscellaneous Collections which have been examined. Translated into English,"Cutty Sark" means Short Shirt, or Chemise, and as far as memory serves me, the above setting had been obtained from a comparatively modern manuscript obtained from Sergt. James O'Neill.

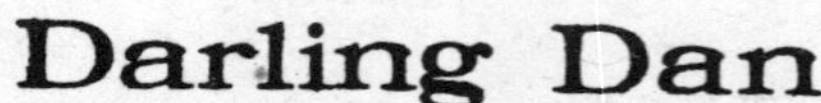

Darling Dan

Rice-Walsh Mss.

292

Crossing the Field

Rice-Walsh Mss.

293

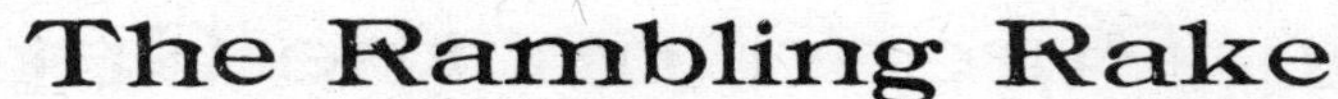

The Rambling Rake

Rice-Walsh Mss.

305

The Cottage in the Grove

Rice-Walsh Mss.

306

The Pigeon on the Gate

"Patsy" Touhey Mss.

307

Altho this splendid reel does not appear in the Bunting, Petrie, or Joyce Collections, it was pretty generally known to the pipers and fiddlers of Chicago, hailing from the west, and south of Ireland and always by the same name. Occasionally variants of the tune are found in Mss. collections. In arrangement, Touhey's setting differs both in key and style from that printed in former O'Neill Collections.

Molly from Longford

"Patsy" Touhey Mss.

308

"Molly" is a variant of "Pay the Girl Her Fourpence" No 804 *O'Neill's Dance Music of Ireland.*

Touhey's Favorite Reel

"Patsy" Touhey. Mss.

309

This is a special setting of "Pat Touhey's Reel" in *O'Neill's Dance Music of Ireland.*

Jenny Dang the Weaver

"Patsy" Touhey. Mss.

310

This old time Scotch reel found in many publications, ancient and modern, first appeared in *Bremner's Collections of Scots Reels or Country Dances 1757.* The version of it as played by the famous "Patsy" Touhey on the Irish or Union pipes, much less cranky than the original and later versions may be found interesting.

The Heel of the Hunt

Capt. F. O'Neill

311

The above reel which is a variant of "The Five-leaved Clover" in former O'Neill Collections, is printed as remembered from boyhood days at the dances, before "patrons" were proscribed.

Paddy McNamara's Reel

Clinton's Irish Melodies 1840

312

Trying to Go to Sleep

Capt. F. O'Neill

313

The Swells of Coolrahan

Pat. Dunne. Mss.

It may be remarked that Mr. Dunne was a farmer of the townland of Kilbraugh not far from Thurles, Tipperary. From his wonderful repertory of dance tunes, generously contributed some years ago, many have been selected.

The Old Maid

Capt. F. O'Neill

The Falls of Doonass

(or Clancy's Reel)

James Clancy. San Francisco.

316

Tom Clair's Maggie

Noted from Clair's playing
by Capt. F. O'Neill.

The first part of Mr. Clair's tune differs but little from "Drowsy Maggie," in common circulation.

Frisky Fanny

Capt. F. O'Neill.

318

"Hoptoun House" as it was then named was first printed in the 9th number of *Robert Bremner's A Collection of Scots Reels, and Country Dances, Edinburgh, 1760*. The Editor has taken the liberty of supplying it with a second finish.

The Sligo Dandy
Patrick Stack—Chicago
321
Fiddlers' Frolic
Patrick Stack—Chicago
322

The Millstone

Wm. McMahon - San Francisco

The Glendowan Reel

An itinerant Kerry fiddler named McKenna, familiarly called "Kennaw" who flourished in the latter half of the 19th century was a human "freak" With a huge body balanced on a diminutive pair of legs, he traveled his circuit mounted on a donkey trained to carry him safely up- and down stairways.

The Shaskan Reel

Patrick Stack - Chicago

When John Keegan Casey who died in 1870, author of "Donal Kenny" wrote the opening lines: "Come piper play 'The Shaskan Reel' Or else 'The Lasses on the Heather'" those tunes were obviously old, altho' they had escaped the vigilance of the great collectors Bunting, Petrie, and Joyce. "The Shaskan Reel" or "Shaskeen Reel" as it has been introduced to us by John McFadden a clever traditional fiddler of the Irish Music Club of Chicago, was printed for the first time in the O'Neill Collections. After being given publicity it won immediate popularity, and soon was a best seller among phonograph records. Like other traditional tunes it has since been subjected to various changes and embellishments at the hands of clever musicians as displayed in the florid variant developed by the versatile "Paddy Stack." To illustrate the wealth of graces, turns, and trills, which adorn the performance of capable Irish pipers and fiddlers, skilful both in execution and improvisation is beyond the scope of exact musical notation. And by the way Stack is an engineer, and not a professional musician.

327

The Rose in Full Bloom

H. Hudson Mss. 1840-41
From Sullivan a famous piper

328

Farewell to Connacht

John Kelly- San Francisco

329

The Scholar

(A Variant with three parts)

John Kelly, San Francisco

330

Long before I had any idea of publishing a work of this character, the fame of John Kelly, and Joseph P. Tamony, as phenomenal fiddlers, had reached Chicago. The measured score of their tunes, for which I am indebted to our mutual friend Francis E. Walsh of San Francisco, is incapable of doing justice to the spirit and excellence of their execution, for all gifted Irish musicians instinctively embellish their performance with peculiar trills, turns and graces, more easily recognized than described.

"The Scholar" was first printed in *Levey's Dance Music of Ireland vol I London 1858;* and not since then until the publication of the O'Neill Collections in recent years. The tune seems to have been a favorite with the fiddlers and pipers of Longford, Leitrim, and Roscommon, as early as the second quarter of the 19th century; and by the way, our talented contributor Mr Kelly hails from the latter county.

The Leinster Hornpipe

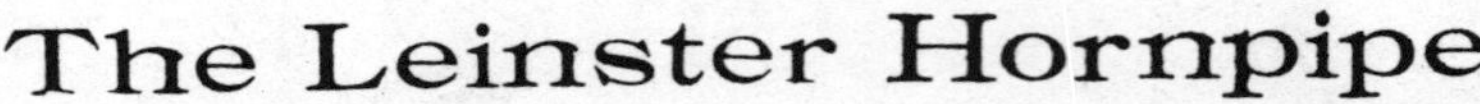

Francis E. Walsh, San Francisco

331

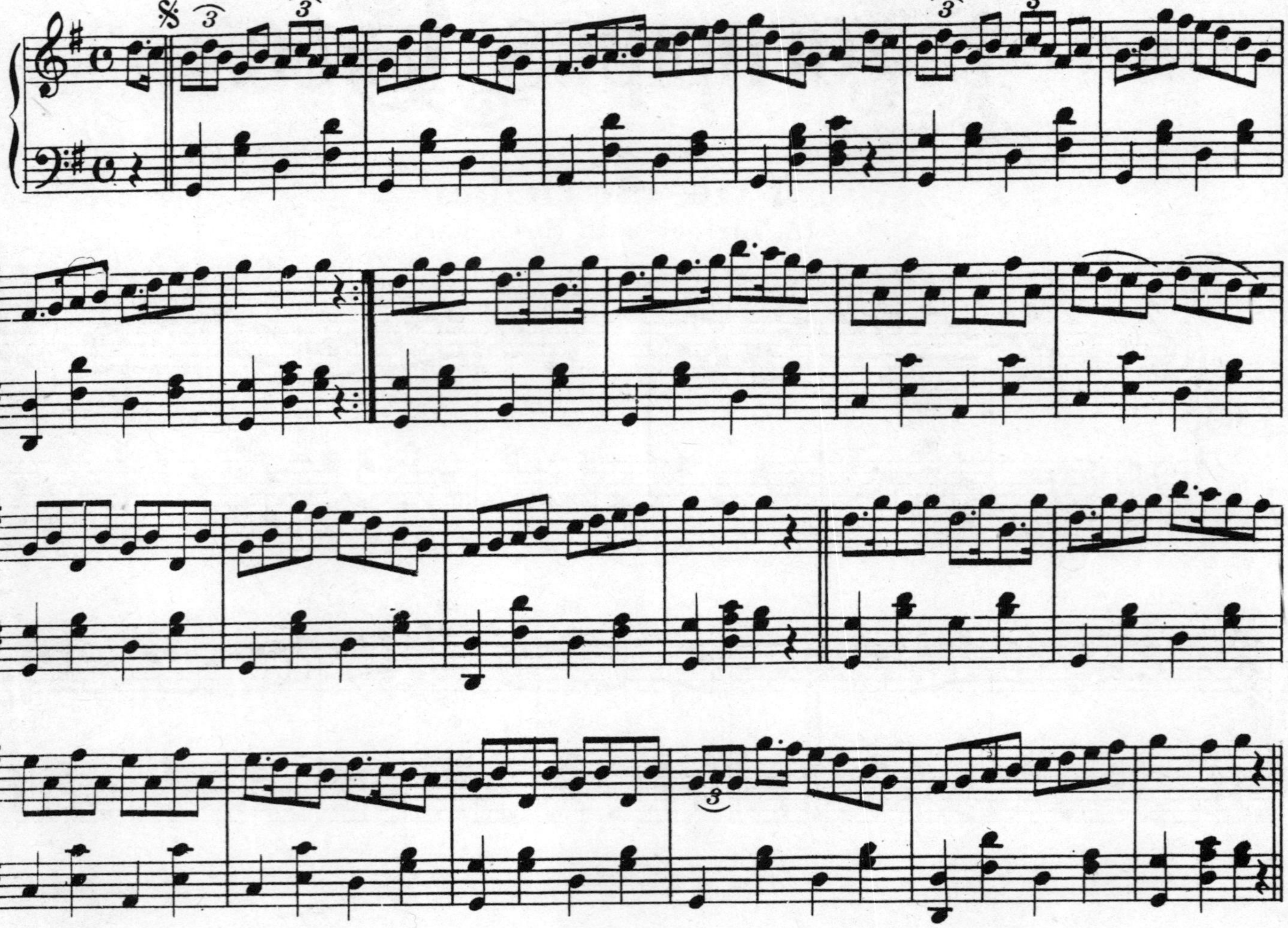

Tamony's Hornpipe

Joseph P. Tamony, San Francisco

332

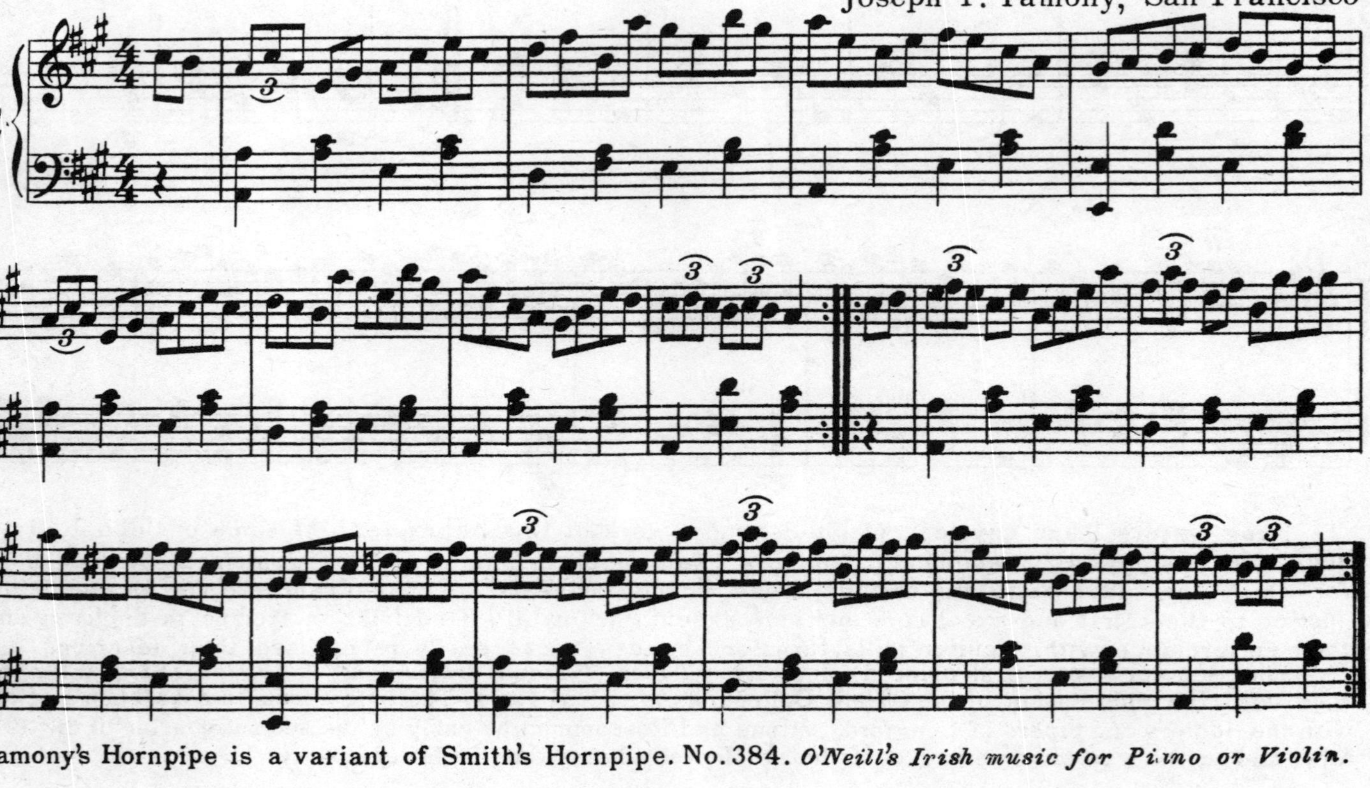

Tamony's Hornpipe is a variant of Smith's Hornpipe. No. 384. *O'Neill's Irish music for Piano or Violin.*

* Dan Lowry was a Dublin theatrical man

The Knuckeen Free

Capt. F. O'Neill

336

In the days of our fathers, *"An Chnoicin Fraoich,"* or "The Little Heathy Hill," both as song and air enjoyed no little popularity in the province of Munster, particularly in the counties of Cork and Kerry. As an air several settings of the melody have been printed, but never as a hornpipe until now, and under its colloquial name among the peasantry.

It wili be remembered that many notable dance tunes, especially hornpipes and long dances have been derived from song airs, such as "The Blackbird," "The Job of Journeywork," "The Garden of Daisies," "Rodney's Glory," and many others.

Stack's Hornpipe

Patrick Stack, Chicago

337

This tune is a variant of "The Cloone Hornpipe" published in *O'Neill's Music of Ireland, 1903,* and *O'Neill's Dance Music of Ireland 1907.* It was obtained from Sergt. James Early who learned it from his tutor on the Union Pipes "Old Man" Quinn. Like many other fine tunes it was anonymous, so it was named "The Cloone Hornpipe" in honor of the famous piper's native town and parish in county Leitrim, Ireland.

Its continued popularity is evidenced by its inclusion in a recent Irish Collection under the identical name invented for it by its sponsor, Sergt. James Early of Chicago.

Shuter's Hornpipe

Wilson's Companion to the Ballroom. 1816

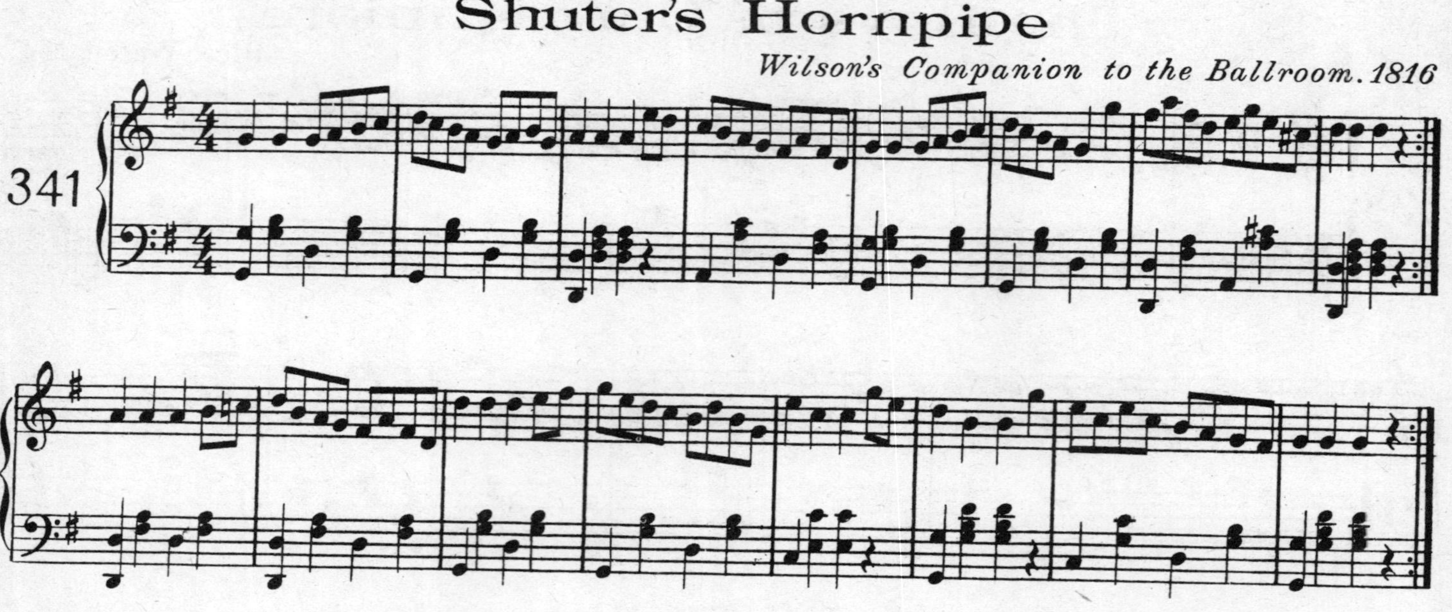

The Devonshire Hornpipe

Wilson's Companion to the Ballroom. 1816

The Dorsetshire Hornpipe

Wilson's Companion to the Ballroom. 1816

Whiteside's Hornpipe
James Whiteside, Mss.
344
Boys of Ballycastle
Pat Dunne Mss.
345
Shanahan's Hornpipe
Prof. P. D. Reidy, Mss.
346

Miss Carroll's Hornpipe
O'Farrell's National Irish Music 1797
347
The Spry Young Lad
Capt. F. O'Neill
348
Mc Nally's Hornpipe
Capt. F. Neill
349

Lucy Campbell's Hornpipe

Rice-Walsh Mss.

350

A Stage Hornpipe

Rice-Walsh, Mss.

351

Egan's Hornpipe

Rice-Walsh, Mss.

352

Mrs. Wilson's Hornpipe

Richer's Hornpipe

Wilson's Companion to the Ballroom. 1816

Astley's Hornpipe

Wilson's Companion to the Ballroom. 1816

The Merry Man Hornpipe

Wilson's Companion to the Ballroom. 1816

The Liscarroll Hornpipe
Jerry O'Reilly San Francisco
358
Jack O'Neill's Fancy
John E. O'Neill, Chicago
359

Miss Rochelle Rudolph's Hornpipe

Patrick O'Leary—Adelaide, Australia

360
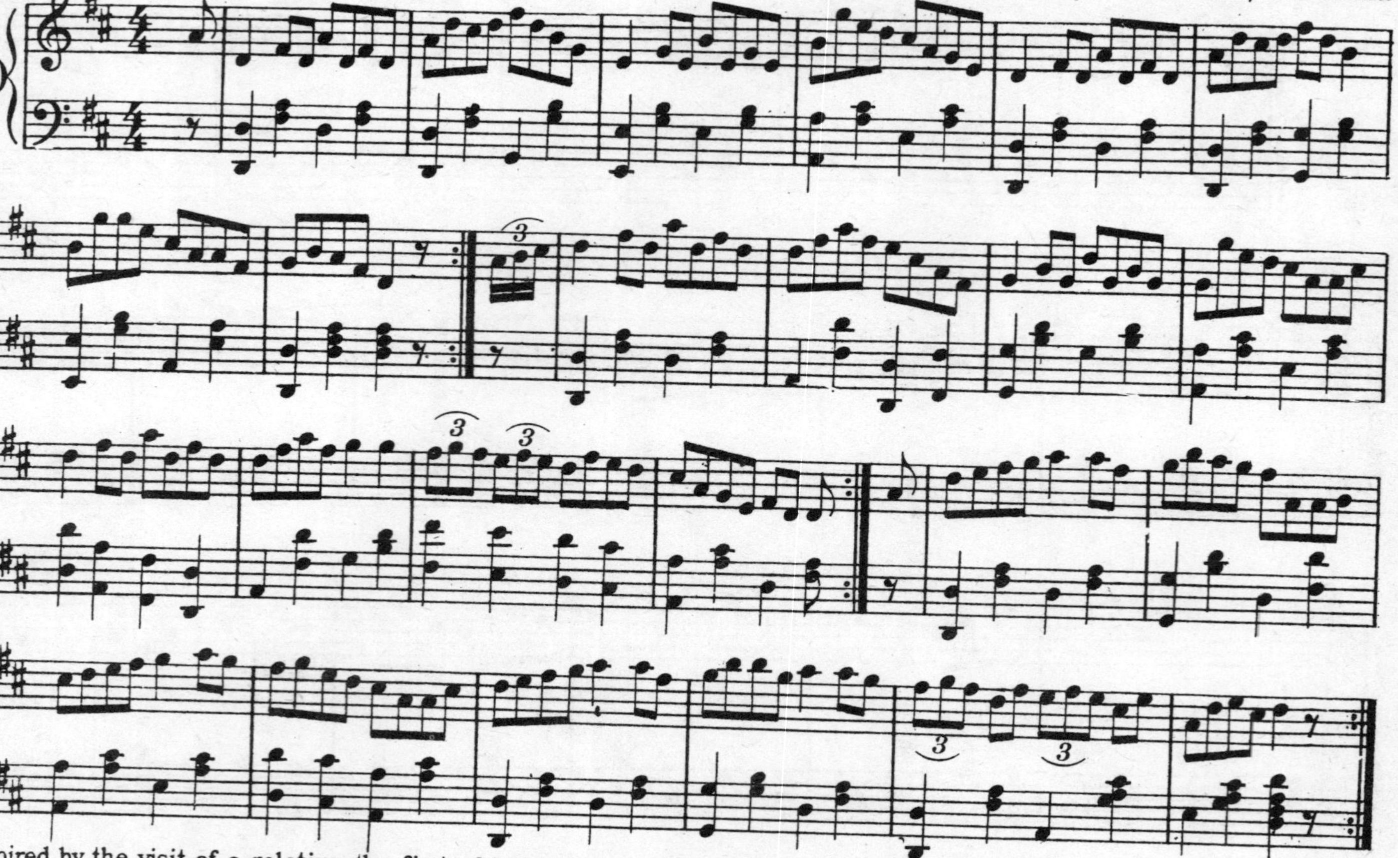

Inspired by the visit of a relative, the first of his blood to greet him at the antipodes, since as a youth he left his native Cavan, Mr. O'Leary commemorated the occasion by the composition of this fine hornpipe in her name. A sketch of his life in "Some Famous Fiddlers" pages 379 to 384, *Irish Minstrels and Musicians* will amply repay perusal.

Moran's Hornpipe

Patrick Stack— Chicago

361

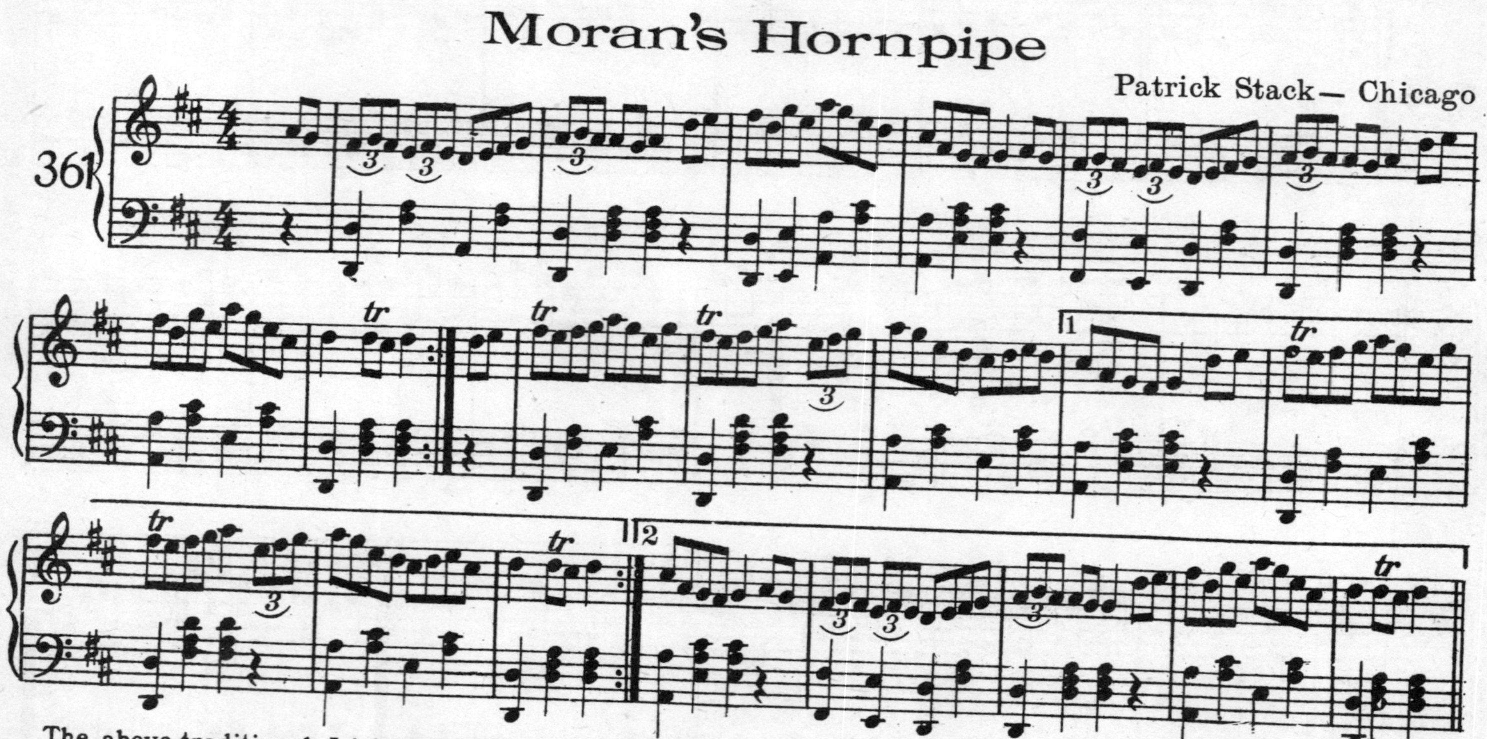

The above traditional Irish hornpipe now printed for the first time, circulated without a name among the fiddlers around Listowell, County Kerry, in Stack's student days. The present title is that by which it has been given publicity by Michael J. Gallagher a clever performer on the Irish or Union pipes, recently from Ireland.

HORNPIPE

Raftery's Favorite

When the slumbering memory of Edward Cronin of the Irish Music Club of Chicago was aroused after his discovery at the beginning of this Century, many a rare dance tune flowed from his facile fingers; among them being a variant of "Raftery's Favorite." Being anonymous like so many others of his repertory it was named "Limerick Junction"- Mr. Cronin's native town in North Tipperary.

Little can be said of this strain, except that it is neither ancient nor really modern- It dates back at least half a century when songs and parodies were sung to it. Being in good hornpipe, or rather clog rhythm it may be regarded as worthy of preservation.

The Ewe with the Crooked Horn

Edw. Cronin – Tipperary

The origin of this unique name, the memory of which is but little more than legendary in our day, has been definitely traced back to the 18th century. A nameless reel known to a few aged members of the Irish Music Club of Chicago, was called "Cronin's Favorite," printed with his two variations in *O'Neill's Music of Ireland, (1903),* and reprinted four years later in *The Dance Music of Ireland,* as "The Flowers of Limerick" its alleged proper name. In the *Stanford-Petrie Complete Collection of Irish Music, London, 1902-5;* we find that No. 918 "The Ewe with the Crooked Horn— a Cork reel. From P. Carew's M.S." is a variant of Edward Cronin's tune. In a footnote we read, "Petrie adds 'hornpipe' in pencil."

Following is a distinct tune of almost identical name found in *Wood's Songs of Scotland, Edinburgh, 1848;* with a long rhyming tribute in the Scottish vernacular, to the admirable qualites of "The Ewie wi' the Crookit Horn," from the pen of "the Rev. Mr. John Skinner." The editor, Farquhar Graham informs us in a footnote that "the verses are adapted to a fine lively Highland reel of considerable antiquity which received its name from a 'Ewie' of a very different breed; namely, the whisky-still with its crooked, or rather spiral apparatus." The figurative significance of the name originated by the Rev. Song writer about the year 1780, caught the popular fancy, and soon found its way into Ireland. The melodies or tunes associated with it serve to perpetuate its memory, while "Carron's Reel" the original name of the Scotch tune is no longer heard.

The Ewie wi' the Crookit Horn

Wood's Songs of Scotland, Edinburgh, 1848